This book employs a
simple rating system to
help choose which
places to visit:

  do not miss

  see if you can

  worth seeing if
you have time

INTRODUCTION

Reaching for the skies: a forest of Vancouver skyscrapers and yachts

INTRODUCTION

Vancouver is spectacular by nature and by design. Commonly called the gateway to the Pacific, it is almost entirely surrounded by water. To the north is Burrard Inlet, a large ice-free harbour, where anchored freighters fly flags from many nations. To the south, the city is stopped near the airport by the north arm of the Fraser River. The Fraser flows west into the Strait of Georgia, which separates Vancouver and the rest of the mainland from Vancouver Island.

As one prairie farmer wryly remarked, 'Vancouver would be great, if the view wasn't blocked by the mountains.' The northern backdrop of Hollyburn, Grouse and Seymour mountains keeps the biting Arctic winds at bay. But this same sheltering sierra attracts huge grey clouds which shower the city with an average of 50 inches (140cm) of rain a year, mostly in winter. This results in perhaps the freshest air on the continent and lush green

Essential
Vancouver and
British Columbia

by

CAROL BAKER

Carol Baker is an experienced travel writer. She and her
husband live in Vancouver, where they run a creative
communications company.

AA

Produced by the Publishing Division of
The Automobile Association

Written by Carol Baker
Peace and Quiet section by Paul Sterry
Consultant: Frank Dawes

Edited, designed and produced by the Publishing Division of The Automobile Association. Maps © The Automobile Association 1991

Distributed in the United Kingdom by the Publishing Division of The Automobile Association, Fanum House, Basingstoke, Hampshire, RG21 2EA

A CIP catalogue record for this book is available from the British Library.

ISBN 0 7495 0085 9

Published by The Automobile Association

Typesetting: Tradespools Ltd, Frome, Somerset

Colour separation: — BTB Repro Whitchurch Hampshire.

Printed in Italy by Printers S.R.L., Trento

Front cover picture: Canada Place

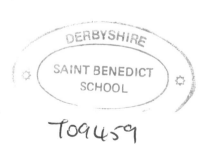

landscapes all year round, except for the occasional winter when a shawl of gentle snow wraps the city in white and creates chaos on the streets. Although clouds frost the coastal mountains with enough snow for good city skiing five months a year, the temperate climate is largely responsible for the profusion of flowers. Daffodils and crocuses emerge in February, followed by the blossoms of Japanese cherry and other flowering trees. May and June bring rhododendrons and azaleas, and roses are blooming much of the year. In autumn, the maples, birches and other deciduous trees drop their tinted red and amber leaves, while the burnt sienna-barked arbutus stays green all year.

Metropolitan Vancouver stretches 1,076 square miles (2,787 sq km) in area, mostly south and east. Suburbs include North Vancouver, West Vancouver, and Lion's Bay across the Lion's Gate Bridge; Burnaby, Coquitlam, Port Coquitlam, Port Moody, Pitt Meadows and Maple Ridge to

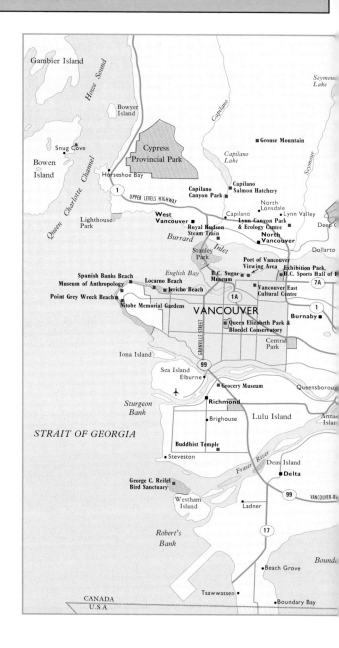

Gambier Island

Howe Sound

Seymour Lake

Bowyer Island

Capilano

Snug Cove

Cypress Provincial Park

■ Grouse Mountain

Capilano Lake

Bowen Island

Horseshoe Bay

Seymour

UPPER LEVELS HIGHWAY

Capilano Canyon Park ■

Capilano Salmon Hatchery ■

Lighthouse Park

West Vancouver ■

Royal Hudson Steam Train ■

Capilano

North Lonsdale

Lynn Valley

Lynn Canyon Park & Ecology Centre

Deep C

Burrard Inlet

North Vancouver

Dollarto

Stanley Park

English Bay

Port of Vancouver Viewing Area

Exhibition Park, ■ B.C. Sports Hall of I

Spanish Banks Beach ■

Locarno Beach ■

B.C. Sugar Museum ■

Museum of Anthropology ■

Jericho Beach ■

Point Grey Wreck Beach ■

Vancouver East Cultural Centre ■

7A

Nitobe Memorial Gardens ■

1A

VANCOUVER

Queen Elizabeth Park & Bloedel Conservatory ■

Burnaby ■

1

Iona Island

GRANVILLE STREET

Central Park

99

Sea Island Elburne ■

■ Grocery Museum

Queensborou

Sturgeon Bank

✈

Richmond ■

STRAIT OF GEORGIA

Brighouse ■

Lulu Island

Anna Islan

Buddhist Temple ■

Fraser River

Steveston ■

Deas Island

■ Delta

George C. Reifel Bird Sanctuary ■

99

VANCOUVER-BL

Westham Island

Ladner ■

17

Robert's Bank

Boundo

Beach Grove ■

CANADA U.S.A.

Tsawwassen ■

Boundary Bay ■

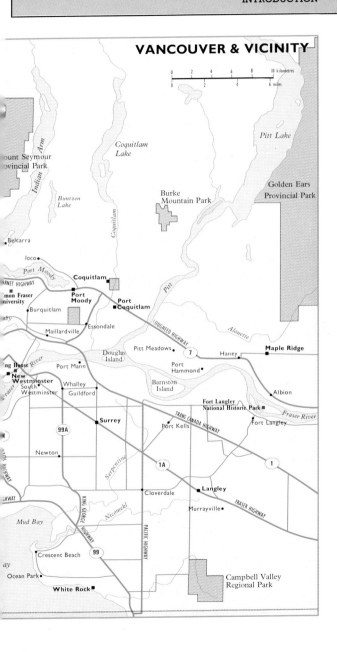

VANCOUVER & VICINITY

0   2   4   6   8   10 kilometres

0   2   4   6 miles

Coquitlam Lake

Pitt Lake

ount Seymour
ovincial Park

Indian Arm

Burke
Mountain Park

Golden Ears
Provincial Park

Buntzen Lake

Coquitlam

• Belcarra

• Ioco

Port Moody

ARNET HIGHWAY

■ Coquitlam

mon Fraser
niversity

■ Port
Moody

Pitt

■ Port
Coquitlam

by

• Burquitlam

LOUGHEED HIGHWAY

Alouette

Maillardville •

• Essondale

Douglas
Island

Pitt Meadows •

7

Haney •

■ Maple Ridge

ng House River

• Port Mann

Port
Hammond •

■
New
Westminster

• Whalley

South
Westminster

• Guildford

Barnston
Island

• Albion

Fort Langley
National Historic Park ■

Fraser River

■ Surrey

Port Kells •

TRANS CANADA HIGHWAY

Fort Langley •

99A

Newton •

Serpentine

1A

1

■ Langley

Mud Bay

KING GEORGE HIGHWAY

Nicomekl

Cloverdale •

Murrayville •

FRASER HIGHWAY

PACIFIC HIGHWAY

GHWAY

• Crescent Beach

99

Campbell Valley
Regional Park

ay

Ocean Park •

■ White Rock

the east; Richmond, White Rock and Delta to the south; and New Westminster, Surrey and Langley to the southeast.

Although Vancouver (metropolitan population: 1.5 million) is Canada's third largest centre (after Toronto and Montreal), the city appears uncrowded most of the time. It is probably the many waterways, forested mountains and plethora of parks that lend the illusion of space. This 'village on the edge of the rainforest', as Vancouver has been affectionately called, is becoming more cosmopolitan every minute. The potpourri of people includes British (700,000), Chinese (100,000), German (80,000), French (50,000) and substantial numbers of Scandinavian, East Indian, native Indian, Italian, Japanese, Greek, and Vietnamese residents. This dynamic and growing cultural mix has resulted in a startling cornucopia of cuisines, art and entertainment from around the world, and an international collection of goods, both downtown and in sprawling suburban shopping centres. The continuing injection of money and talent from around the globe has helped create a thriving economy. Although Vancouver's past has largely been the story of seeking and selling such natural resources as lumber, fish and minerals, new industries are emerging. Citizen skills now produce sightseeing submarines, satellite-sensing equipment, computer software and data terminal designs. These enhance a growing tourism industry, which draws some visitors back as residents. British Columbia receives 13,000,000 visitors annually, who contribute C$3.2 billion to provincial coffers. Vancouver harbour handles 150,000 cruise ship passengers.

Provincial ferries carry close to seven million vehicles and 17 million passengers each year. Superb hotels continue to spring up in a city centre of skyscrapers of steel, marble, chrome and glass, punctuated by patches of demolition and excavation to make room for more modern buildings. Well-developed facilities and roadways allow visitors and residents to ski in the morning, sail in the afternoon and enjoy opera in the evening. Even business seems to be a sport in this city, which boasts one of the most speculative stock markets in the world.

BACKGROUND

A mere 200 years ago, Salish Indians lived here in scattered villages, moving from place to place in small canoes or paddling quietly through the forests. Indians of other tribes came seasonally to the mouth of the Fraser, where salmon choked the river. Fish were so plentiful that at times they could be scooped by hand from the water.

In 1791 the first foreigners, a small Spanish exploration party, came floating in to what is now known as Spanish Banks, and nothing was ever the same again. In exchange for a gift of salmon, they taught the awe-struck local natives a popular European tune, known today as 'For He's A Jolly Good Fellow'. A year later, Captain George Vancouver arrived and named Point Grey, Robert's Bank and Burrard Inlet, but within weeks his two ships sailed away, leaving behind forever the site of the city that would be named after him.

The Fraser River's name commemorates trader Simon Fraser, who paid a brief and hazardous call to the area in the early 19th century

No more Europeans appeared until 1808, when Yankee trader Simon Fraser came looking for fur routes. After a perilous journey down a turbulent river, he arrived at a village of

An active tongue and a keen ambition earned John Deighton his reputation as Gassy Jack

Musqueam Indians, who chased him and his men back upstream. His visit lasted about an hour. But his name stayed—for a river, a street and a university. A plaque on the road near the University of British Columbia marks that brief and hostile meeting.

In 1827, the Hudson's Bay Company approached from the east and established a trading post for natives at Fort Langley. The fort, which was never engaged in hostilities, had been built to impress Americans who had been casting covetous eyes towards this part of the continent. A gold rush on the Fraser in the 1850s saw a flood of 25,000 prospectors, mostly from California. Consequently a nervous government in London established the Colony of British Columbia, a name chosen by Queen Victoria. Roads were built and the first one, North Road, is still the boundary between the suburbs of Burnaby and Coquitlam. A trail was blazed from the colony capital, New Westminster, to Burrard Inlet to provide an ice-free harbour in case the Fraser River should ever freeze (and it did, two years later). In 1862, the McCleery family established a farm on the north bank of the Fraser, becoming the first settlers on the land now within a city. Shortly thereafter, Yorkshireman John Morton saw a chunk of coal from Burrard Inlet in a shop window. Morton came from a family of potters and knew that near coal there is often clay, and clay meant bricks. An Indian guide led Morton to the coal seam in what is now Coal Harbour. He found no clay, but in partnership with two friends, bought 500 acres (200 hectares) of nearby land for $1.01 an acre, and became the butt of jokes in New Westminster for buying such remote and useless acreage. The men were nicknamed the Three Greenhorns. That land today is the high-rise apartment-studded West End, whose current value totals billions of dollars.

The towering trees that loomed over tiny Indian settlements and the lonesome tents and sheds of the early settlers led to early prosperity. Lumber companies cut and shipped the trees, many more than 300 feet (100m) high. The quality of Burrard Inlet lumber soon became world famous, and massive beams, 20 inches (50cm) square and 70 feet (21m) long without a single knot were shipped around the globe. Some are in the Imperial Palace in Beijing.

In 1867, a garrulous Yorkshireman named John Deighton proposed a saloon on Burrard Inlet for mill workers. The workers pieced together the rickety establishment within 24 hours. Their enthusiasm was not surprising, since the alternative was a 15 mile (24km) hike through a forest full of bears to New Westminster. Deighton, who had arrived with his wife, six dollars in cash, a few sticks of furniture and a yellow dog, was an overnight success. Because he was so talkative and optimistic about prospects for the inlet, locals called him 'Gassy Jack', and the ramshackle collection of huts and shops surrounding his saloon was dubbed Gastown. His statue stands in Maple Leaf Square in Gastown today. The mill store is Vancouver's oldest building, although it was moved by barge a few decades ago to Pioneer Park at the north end of Alma Street, where it operates today as a tiny museum.

In 1871 British Columbia joined Confederation

and Vancouverites could call themselves Canadians.

A bridge, a school and a hotel were soon built. By 1881 the population of Gastown was about 200, but wives, children, Indians, Orientals and prostitutes were not counted. When in 1879, the federal government selected Burrard Inlet as the western terminus of the new coast-to-coast Canadian Pacific Railway, land speculation exploded. CPR Manager William Van Horne visited Gastown (officially named Granville, but everyone called it Gastown) in 1884 and decided the city should be called Vancouver, because the whole European world was aware of Captain Vancouver's explorations, and Van Horne wanted the world to know where the CPR terminus was. Since the CPR was the city's largest landlord, there was little argument. Lauchlan Hamilton surveyed the city centre and named all the streets. Is it coincidence that the first street surveyed is named Hamilton?

The city continued to grow. Early in 1886, 500 buildings went up in 75 days. The City of

The Lion's Gate Bridge brought new access and new crowds to the North Shore when it opened in 1938

Vancouver was incorporated on 6 April of that
year, although the ceremony was delayed
because no one remembered to bring a pencil
and paper to record the details. Mayor Malcolm
MacLean and his council soon asked the federal
government to lease back to the city as a park
the military reserve to the west. It had been
established when fears of American
encroachment were very real. Those 1,000 acres
(400 hectares) became Stanley Park, named
after the governor general who opened it.
Shortly thereafter, a sudden squall blew a scrub
fire towards the city. Within an hour, the
thousand or so ramshackle buildings that made
up the two-month-old city were almost all
destroyed by fire, and about 20 people died. But
citizens began to rebuild while the ashes were
still warm. The following year, the first Hotel
Vancouver opened, and the first passenger train
from Montreal was met by a huge and jubilant
crowd. By 1888 the population totalled 8,000 and
there were 36 miles (58km) of plank roads and
24 miles (38km) of wooden sidewalks. The next
year culture came to Vancouver with a
presentation of Shakespeare's *Richard III* in the
Imperial Opera House. By 1890 the population
reached 12,500 and electric streetcars started
running. The Anglo-British Packing Company
opened and eventually became the largest
sockeye-packing company in the world. In 1891,
CPR Empress Line steamships began their
storied stops at Vancouver. That same year, the
Nine O'Clock Gun was installed in Stanley Park,
and still booms out a time signal at nine each
evening.
During the boom of 1912–13, buildings went up
and prices soared as properties changed hands
at a dizzying pace. The city economy got another
boost in 1918 with the opening of the Panama
Canal: low-cost wheat shipments became
possible in much shorter times. In 1923 Warren
Harding came to Vancouver, the first American
president to visit Canada. The local Kiwanis
Club erected a monument to him, in Stanley
Park, sculpted by Charles Margea, who also
created the lions at the south end of the Lion's
Gate Bridge. When the bridge opened in 1938,
thanks to the Guinness family, the population of
the North Shore exploded.

BACKGROUND

Vancouver's high-rise buildings bathe in reflected glory

In 1939 an aquarium opened, the forerunner of today's splendid aquatic collection in Stanley Park. By 1940 Vancouver boasted the busiest airport in Canada, with a take-off and landing every 81 minutes during daylight hours. That same year Theatre Under The Stars (TUTS), which still runs in Stanley Park, began (see **Nightlife and Entertainment**, page 86). During the 1950s, Vancouverites saw their first 3-D film; the BC Lions and the Calgary Stampeders attracted 28,000 fans, the largest crowd to date to watch a football game in Canada; and Bill Haley and the Comets brought rock and roll to Vancouver. The 1960s and '70s brought the Beatles, television, luxurious hotels, another university, a planetarium and the Museum of Anthropology. In 1983 the dome roof was inflated on BC Place Stadium. Three years later the international trade fair, EXPO 86, welcomed the world and put Vancouver firmly on the global list of great places.

WHAT TO SEE

Before setting out, it is wise to find a reference point. Assuming that the city is not hiding under a cloak of heavy clouds or rain, the Cypress Bowl, Grouse and Seymour mountains indicate north. Several sites provide an eagle's eye view of downtown and environs. The glass elevators on the south side of Harbour Centre at 555 West Hastings Street (tel: 689-0421) run up 553 feet (167m) to a revolving restaurant and an observation deck. The price of a meal and a drink at Cloud Nine, atop the 42-storey Sheraton Hotel at 1400 Robson Street (tel: 687-0511) includes a 360 degree view of the city. Gourmets love the revolving restaurant at the top of the New World Harbourside Hotel. If heights make you dizzy, then head for Canada Place, with its spectacular five white sails, a city landmark at the north end of Burrard Street, where a stroll alongside the cruise ship moorages, on the outdoor promenade deck, passes a dozen landmarks pointing out sites of interest around the city.

Art Galleries and Museums

Vancouver's comparatively young art colony is fresh with enthusiasm and is gaining renown on the international scene. Local galleries display old European and Asian masters, the Canadian Group of Seven, Eskimo sculptures of soapstone, whalebone and ivory, the colourful and abstract woodcarvings and paintings of native Indians, and the contemporary works of painters, sculptors and photographers. Local greats include Emily Carr, Fred Varley, BC. Binning, Jack Shadbolt, Charles Hepburn Scott, Gordon Smith, Lawren Harris, Alistair Bell, Bill Reid, Toni Onley and Robert Young.

Past and future: Vancouver's Museum and Planetarium

HR MACMILLAN PLANETARIUM

1100 Chestnut Street
Entertaining and educational programmes varying from astronomy shows to laser shows.
Open: Tuesday to Sunday.
Shows at 14.30 and 20.00 hrs; additional shows at 13.00 and 16.00 hrs on weekends and holidays.
From the nearby **Gordon Southam Observatory**, you can

observe the sun, moon, stars, comets, planets and galaxies, and NASA mission broadcasts when possible.
Open: Friday to Sunday (Tuesday to Sunday in July and August) 12.00–17.00 hrs and 19.00–23.00 hrs. Observatory hours vary.

MUSEUM OF ANTHROPOLOGY
6393 North West Marine Drive (on the UBC campus)
In the Great Hall, natural light streams through 45-foot (14m)-high windows to illumine an exquisite collection of elegant soaring cedar totem poles, red cedar chests and carved canoes and dishes. The Masterpiece Gallery houses an intriguing collection of intricately-carved miniatures in silver, gold, bone, argillite and wood. The massive sculpture *The Raven and the First Man*, carved in yellow cedar by Haida artist Bill Reid,

highlights the contemporary collection. About 90 per cent of the museum's collection of Northwest Coast Indian and other art and artefacts is on view, thanks to several series of glass-topped drawers.
Open: Tuesday to Sunday 11.00–17.00 hrs; hours extended Tuesdays to 21.00 hrs; closed Mondays, and 25 and 26 December

◆
VANCOUVER ART GALLERY
750 Hornby Street
The neoclassical heritage building, once home to the provincial law courts and a work of art in itself, shelters works by the Canadian Group of Seven, the evocative rainforest works of Emily Carr (1871–1945, British Columbia's most talented artist to date), works by Dutch, Italian,

Graceful totems eye each other in the Museum of Anthropology

French, German and English masters, photography, sculpture, graphics and video works. You can wander around on your own or join a free 20-minute tour. The reference-only library, a gift shop and restaurant render the Vancouver Art Gallery a rainy-day special.
Open: Monday to Saturday 10.00–17.00 hrs; hours extended to 21.00 hrs on Thursdays; Sundays 12.00–17.00 hrs. Free Tuesdays and Thursdays from 17.00 hrs. Closed Tuesdays in autumn and winter

◆◆
VANCOUVER MARITIME MUSEUM
1905 Ogden Avenue
This museum, identified by a tall Kwakiutl totem in front, highlights the history of marine exploration, sailing, fishing, maritime art and the developments of the port of Vancouver. Near by is the *St Roch*, an official national historic site. The two-masted schooner, built in the 1920s as an RCMP ship, became the first vessel to navigate through the treacherous Northwest Passage west to east (in 1928–29).
Open: daily 10.00–17.00 hrs. Closed Christmas Day. Tours every 30 minutes

◆
VANCOUVER MUSEUM
1100 Chestnut Street
This museum is devoted to the history of Vancouver and the native peoples of the northwest, and also houses a collection of decorative arts from Asia, Europe and the Americas.
Open: daily 10.00–17.00 hrs; hours extended Monday to

Friday to 21.00 hrs in summer. Closed Mondays September to May and Christmas Day

Other Galleries
While most private galleries are in the South Granville area between 6th and 15th Avenues, new galleries have been opening along West Georgia and Beatty streets. The **Bau-Xi Gallery** at 3045 Granville Street (tel: 733-7011) features contemporary Canadian Art. The **Buschlen Mowatt Gallery** at 1445 West Georgia Street (tel: 682-1234) houses expensive contemporary international art. The **Diane Farris Gallery** at 1565 West Seventh Avenue (tel: 737-2629) exhibits and sells mostly avant-garde works. The **Equinox Gallery** at 2321 Granville Street (tel: 736-2405) houses contemporary international art and photographic shows. The **Heffel Gallery**, at 2247 Granville Street (tel: 732-6505), specialises in the Group of Seven and other well-established Canadian and international artists. For native Indian and Inuit art, **Images for a Canadian Heritage** at 779 Burrard Street (tel: 685-7046) sells a variety of collectables as well as Inuit soapstone carvings and prints and Indian wood carvings, and the **Inuit Gallery** at 345 Water Street (tel: 688-7323) in Gastown, sells many *chef d'oeuvres*. These galleries are usually open Monday to Saturday 10.00–1700 hrs. Some stay open until 18.00 hrs. And the Buschlen Mowatt Gallery, Images for a Canadian Heritage and Inuit Gallery open in the afternoon on Sundays from noon to 17.00 hrs.

WHAT TO SEE – VANCOUVER

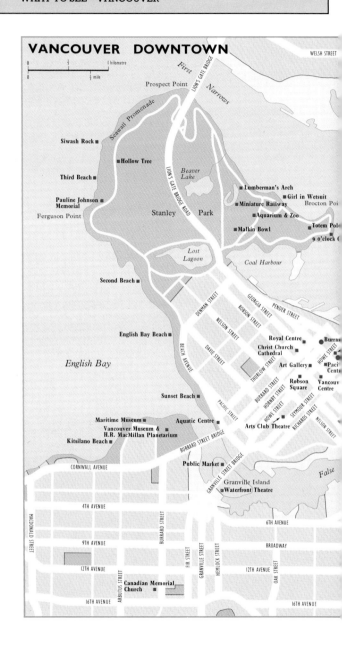

VANCOUVER DOWNTOWN

WELSH STREET

First Narrows

LION'S GATE BRIDGE

Prospect Point

Scawall Promenade

Siwash Rock ■

■ Hollow Tree

Beaver Lake

Third Beach ■

LION'S GATE BRIDGE ROAD

■ Lumberman's Arch

■ Girl in Wetsuit

Pauline Johnson Memorial

■ Miniature Railway

Brocton Poi

Ferguson Point

Stanley   Park

■ Aquarium & Zoo

■ Malkin Bowl

■ Totem Pole

9 o'clock C

Lost Lagoon

Coal Harbour

Second Beach ■

DENMAN STREET

GEORGIA STREET

ROBSON STREET

PENDER STREET

English Bay Beach ■

NELSON STREET

Royal Centre ■

Burra

HOWE STREET

Christ Church Cathedral

BEACH AVENUE

DAVIE STREET

THURLOW STREET

Art Gallery ■

Paci Cent

English Bay

Robson Square

Vancouv Centre

BURRARD STREET

HORNBY STREET

Sunset Beach ■

PACIFIC STREET

HOWE STREET

SEYMOUR STREET

RICHARDS STREET

NELSON STREET

Maritime Museum ■

Aquatic Centre ■

Arts Club Theatre ■

Vancouver Museum & H.R. MacMillan Planetarium ■

Kitsilano Beach ■

BURRARD STREET BRIDGE

CORNWALL AVENUE

Public Market ■

GRANVILLE STREET BRIDGE

False

Granville Island

■ Waterfront Theatre

MACDONALD STREET

4TH AVENUE

BURRARD STREET

6TH AVENUE

FIR STREET

9TH AVENUE

GRANVILLE STREET

HEMLOCK STREET

BROADWAY

12TH AVENUE

12TH AVENUE

OAK STREET

ARBUTUS STREET

16TH AVENUE

Canadian Memorial Church ■

16TH AVENUE

Visual arts in cafés and restaurants has recently become more popular. The **Alma Street Café** at 2502 Alma Street (tel: 222-2244) decorates its walls with good works of art, which are for sale.

Presentation House in North Vancouver and the **Vancouver East Cultural Centre** frequently feature exhibitions of excellent works by Canadian and foreign artists.

Churches

CANADIAN MEMORIAL CHURCH
15th Avenue at Burrard Street
Constructed in greystone gothic style, the Canadian Memorial Church was dedicated in 1928. Its spectacular stained glass windows depict Biblical scenes, Canadian coats of arms and Canadian historical events. The Yukon window illustrates the Chilcoot Pass in 1898, complete with a depiction of a Royal Mail sled.
Open: by appointment

◆
CHRIST CHURCH CATHEDRAL
690 Burrard Street at Georgia Street
Located on a prime piece of real estate, smack in the centre of downtown Vancouver, the 100-year-old Christ Church Cathedral looks as if it should be nestled in a small town in a valley in rural England. Of special interest are the English and Canadian stained glass windows.
Open: Monday to Friday 10.00–16.00 hrs and Sunday 08.00–17.00 hrs

Other Attractions

◆◆◆
AQUARIUM
Stanley Park
Home to 9,000 aquatic creatures, from delicate seahorses to smiling crocodiles, the aquarium's star denizens are the great killer whales who entertain with several daily shows of

One of the main celebrities of Stanley Park's Aquarium – the killer whale, in playful mood

strength and grace. Underwater viewing windows provide ringside seats for the four daily feedings of the much smaller beluga whales.
Open: daily 10.00–17.30 hrs; summer 09.30–20.00 hrs

◆
BC PLACE STADIUM
777 Pacific Boulevard
A Vancouver landmark, this 60,000-seat stadium is the world's largest air-supported dome. Home to the BC Lions football team, the stadium is also the venue for other sporting events, trade shows and concerts.
Open: upon request

◆◆
BUDDHIST TEMPLE
9160 Steveston Highway, Richmond (a 30-minute drive south from downtown)
This exquisite example of Chinese palatial architecture, with golden porcelain tiles and flying rooftop dragons, would be at home on the banks of the Yangtze. The interior is an artistic showcase of eastern sculpture, painting, carpentry and embroidery. An outdoor courtyard encloses a collection of beautiful bonsai plants and a ceramic mural of Kuan-Yin-Bodhisattva.
Open: daily 10.00–17.00 hrs

◆
REIFEL BIRD SANCTUARY
5191 Robertson Road, Delta (a 45-minute drive from downtown)
The swampy delta of the Fraser River boasts the largest and most varied winter bird population in Canada. Bird-watching blinds, benches and numerous pathways through the marshland are popular. February, March and November are especially interesting, thanks to snow geese and other migratory birds.
Open: daily 09.00–16.00 hrs (hours may change; tel: 946-6980 to check)

Science World promises visitors some of the most awe-inspiring images on earth, on the biggest domed screen in the world

◆◆◆
ROYAL HUDSON STEAM TRAIN
BC Rail Station, 1311 West First Street, North Vancouver
One of Canada's few operational steam trains, the Royal Hudson lets you ride back into history. Engine 2860 chugs 40 miles (64km) for the two-hour journey, passing the old cottages and new waterfront mansions of West Vancouver, and along rugged Howe Sound north to the logging town of Squamish. An optional return aboard the MV *Britannia* makes a wonderful excursion; the frosted mountains, lush rainforests, waterways and islands take on different character from land and sea.
If you prefer, you can make the outward journey by boat and return by train.
Departures: Wednesday to Sunday 10.30 from North Vancouver, returning at 14.00 hrs from Squamish May, June, July and September; daily in August

◆◆◆
SCIENCE WORLD
1445 Quebec Street, adjacent to the Main Street Skytrain Station
This shimmering silvery geodesic sphere, another city landmark, bills itself as the most curious place on earth. Four galleries of exhibits feature hands-on exploration of scientific and technological principles. You can touch a tornado, stretch an echo, lose your shadow and touch a rock that glows in the dark.
The OMNIMAX theatre (tel: 875-OMNI for show times) surrounds the audience with awesome imagery on the world's largest domed screen. The Bytes Cafeteria provides food for thought.
Open: daily 10.00–1800 hrs

WHAT TO SEE – VANCOUVER

Fish is a favourite Vancouver dish, and the Steveston fish market provides a superb selection

◆◆
STEVESTON
(a 30-minute drive south from downtown)
Once a Japanese fishing village, Steveston is now becoming more of a cultural mosaic. Each morning Japanese, Vietnamese and other Canadians unload and sell their cargoes of salmon, halibut, cod, flounder, prawns and crab. Several little restaurants serve the local catches and small shops sell arts, crafts and other souvenirs. Guided walking tours are available to visitors from the **Steveston Museum** at 3811 Moncton Street.
Open: 09.30–17.00 hrs Monday to Saturday

◆
WESTMINSTER ABBEY
Dewdney Trunk Road, Mission (an hour's drive east of downtown)
This modern Benedictine monastery is both a high school and a degree-granting arts and theological college. The 10 bells of the 160-foot (50m) tower chime for Sunday masses. Resident monks create and restore paintings and other art forms in an atmosphere of peace and tranquillity. Sculptures, stained glass windows and murals decorate the monastery. Overnight rooms are available, as St Benedict believed that there should always be guests at a monastery.
Open: daily 13.30–16.00 hrs (from 14.00 hrs Sunday). Guided tours available. Visitors should dress modestly.

Parks and Gardens

Vancouver has more than 150 parks and gardens. Remember, this is the edge of the rainforest: carry an umbrella, just in case.

◆◆
CYPRESS PROVINCIAL PARK

(a 30-minute drive northwest from downtown)
Like neighbouring Grouse and Seymour mountains, Cypress Bowl is a four-season playground. The Cypress Bowl recreation area has scenic nordic and alpine skiing runs for winter and spring, and superb hiking trails for the warmer months. On a clear day you can see forever. The Black Mountain chairlift, a café, bar and sundeck are open, weather permitting, daily in summer 11.00–17.00 hrs, in winter 08.00–23.00 hrs, and on weekends only from mid-October to late November and from mid-May to 1 July.

A slice of past life in Fort Langley's reconstructed cooperage

◆◆◆
DR. SUN YAT-SEN CLASSICAL CHINESE GARDEN

578 Carrall Street, Chinatown
This pocket of peace, hidden from the bustle of Chinatown by high whitewashed walls, offers a glimpse of the Ming dynasty. The grey volcanic rock highlighting the garden was imported from Suzhou in China. Hourly guided tours explain the Taoist philosophy of ying and yang, and other aspects of the 'Garden of Ease', as it is called in Cantonese.
Open: daily 10.00–19.00 hrs in summer and 10.00–16.30 hrs October to April

◆
FORT LANGLEY NATIONAL HISTORIC PARK

23433 Mavis Street, Fort Langley (a 50-minute drive east from downtown)
Once the Hudson's Bay Company's most important provisioning post in the Pacific Northwest, Fort Langley is billed

as the birthplace of British Columbia. It was here that British Columbia was declared a crown colony in 1858. Within the high wooden walls of the fort, the Big House, the bastion, a cooperage and carpentry shop and a blacksmith's forge have been reconstructed. The original storehouse contains furs, clothing and other supplies used by fur traders, gold miners, Indians and other residents of the mid-19th century. Fort interpreters in period costumes demonstrate pioneer life of that era.
Open: daily 10.00–18.00 hrs mid-May to Labour Day, and 10.00–16.30 hrs Labour Day to mid-May

NITOBE MEMORIAL GARDENS
1903 West Mall, University of British Columbia
This 215 acre (87 hectare) garden, created in 1960, is the most authentic Japanese garden on the continent. In addition to the rock and sand renderings, the cherry blossoms in April or May and the iris blooms in late June are spectacular.
Open: daily 10.00 hrs to dusk

QUEEN ELIZABETH PARK & BLOEDEL CONSERVATORY
33rd Avenue and Cambie Street
This 150 acre (60 hectare) paradise of lawns, trees, shrubs and flowers is located at the highest spot in the city (500 feet/152m), so the views are

Nature dwarfs the city: a view from Queen Elizabeth Park

spectacular. The blossoms are at their best in May and June, when the azaleas and rhododendrons create a kaleidoscope of colour. The conservatory comprises a tropical garden complete with 20 species of colourful birds flying free, and an arid area with a collection of cacti and seasonal floral displays. The park also features sunken gardens, rose gardens, sculpture, a pitch-and-putt golf course and the Seasons Restaurant.
Open: daily 10.00–21.00 hrs in summer and 10.00–17.00 hrs October to mid-April

◆◆◆
STANLEY PARK

This 1,000 acre (400 hectare) park, a few blocks from the city centre, occupies a peninsula

Impressive and imposing totem poles in Stanley Park

extending from the western edge of town into Burrard Inlet. The six-mile-long (9km) paved perimeter path, known as The Seawall, is divided half for walkers and half for cyclists, and a network of forested trails runs throughout the park. Items of interest include the Nine O'Clock Gun, the *Girl in the Wetsuit* statue, totem poles, Siwash Rock, the hollow tree, and poet Pauline Johnson's 'Lost Lagoon'. Stanley Park is also home to tennis courts, a pitch-and-putt golf course, the aquarium (see separate listing), the zoo with its polar bears, playful otters and seals and such superb restaurants as the Beach House and The Teahouse.
Open: daily, 24 hrs

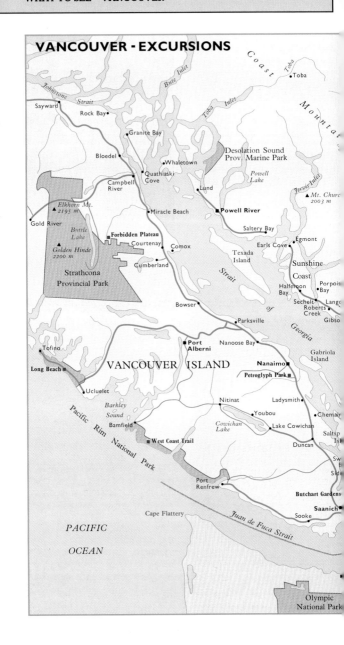

VANCOUVER - EXCURSIONS

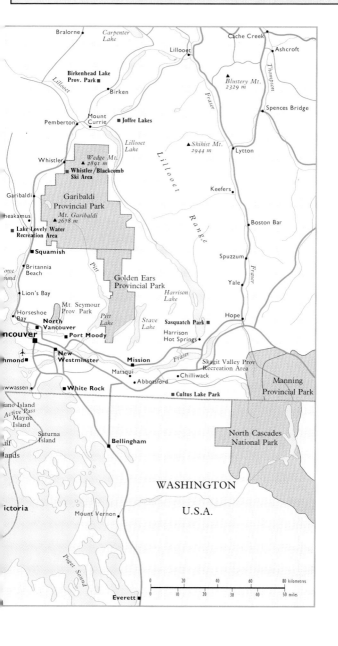

Beaches

Although beachcombing is a pleasant pastime rain or shine in winter, Vancouver beaches are at their best in summer. English Bay, a 15-minute sprint from downtown, sports several superb beaches. At **Sunset Beach**, the closest to downtown, summer sunsets are glorious. If you don't want to watch from a giant log on the beach while the world turns, you can sip a sundowner at the nearby English Bay Café or the Sylvia Hotel, or savour a *souvlaki* at a stand on Beach Avenue.

In Stanley Park, at **Second Beach**, a tidal saltwater pool protects children from the currents and lifeguards monitor the pool mid-June to late August. There are also areas for soccer, football, volleyball, baseball and barbecues. A little farther north, beyond Ferguson Point, lies relatively quiet **Third Beach**. Southwest, beyond the Burrard Street Bridge, **Kitsilano Beach** also has a heated outdoor saltwater pool, overlooking English Bay. Farther along are **Jericho Beach**, **Locarno Beach** and **Spanish Banks**, all favourites with windsurfers and provided with parking, intermittent food stalls and picnic tables.

For unspoiled beauty try **Wreck Beach**, on the tip of the Point Grey Peninsula near the University of British Columbia. This is the only *au naturel* beach in the Lower Mainland, and is accessible via a steep trail winding down to the water from North West Marine Drive.

Suburban Sights

A dozen suburbs offer such varied attractions as the 100-year-old Capilano Suspension Bridge in North Vancouver, and the long, sandy beach in **White Rock**, as well as the examples given under **What to See**, above.

Sun-worshipping on the beach, overlooking English Bay

EXCURSIONS FROM VANCOUVER

GULF ISLANDS

Captain George Vancouver jumped the gun in 1792 when he gave the name Gulf of Georgia to the waters between Vancouver Island and the southwestern mainland of British Columbia. Later explorers discovered that the gulf was not a gulf. It is now called the Strait of Georgia; but its islands are still called the Gulf Islands.

Mayne Island is not the main island. Of the six inhabited Gulf Islands, Saltspring is the most developed and the most densely populated. Mayne Island, about 15 square miles (40 sq km) in area, has only 700 residents, mostly artists and artisans, a few entrepreneurs and some people who survive on savings. The climate is kind: winters are mild, rainfall is about one-third that of Vancouver, and the sun usually shines from April to September. The island is mainly bays and beaches and gentle wooded hills of arbutus, Douglas fir, alder, cedar and brilliant bursts of broom, although early settlers did clear some land for farming. Favoured diversions include swimming, scuba diving, fishing, canoeing, kayaking, clam digging, beachcombing, hiking and cycling; and such pastoral pastimes as watching bald eagles making great circles in the sky before diving for salmon in the Active Pass, or trailing little black-tailed deer. Mayne Island has seen a curious mix of human life in its time. Middens and coarse white beaches formed from eroded clam, abalone and oyster shells indicate that native Indians inhabited Helen Point more than 5,000 years ago. In the 1850s, rowdy miners stopped here *en route* from Victoria to the gold fields of Barkerville, and some returned to enjoy the mild winters. At the turn of the century, British gentry liked to land on Mayne to spend their summers. And when World War II began, one-third of the island residents were Japanese who were cultivating tomatoes with great success. (The Japanese were all relocated a few years later.) Should you decide to join the present-day inhabitants, waterfront lots are currently selling for upwards of C$90,000. The lighthouse at Georgina Point, built in 1855, still guides vessels into the eastern entrance to Active Pass. Current lighthouse keeper Don De Rousie, a Haida Indian, spends his spare time carving yellow and red cedar into classic West Coast Indian designs, and he paints them in traditional reds and blacks. The Mayne Island Gaol, built in 1896, now houses memorabilia, including remnants from the sailing barque *Zephyr*, which hit the Georgina shoals and sank in 1872 (open daily, 10.00–17.00 hrs in summer). Ferries to Mayne Island leave Tsawwassen (an hour's drive south from Vancouver) twice daily.

Accommodation

Although peace pervades the whole island, the snuggest sanctuary of all may be the **Gingerbread House** (tel: 539-3133), a cottage overlooking

EXCURSIONS FROM VANCOUVER

sheltered Campbell Bay.
Originally built in 1900 in classic
Victorian gothic style, the
Gingerbread House was barged
from Vancouver to Mayne Island
a decade ago. Local craftsmen
restored the cottage and present
owners Ken and Karen
Somerville furnished it with
comfortable Victoriana. There
are four guest rooms, and room
rates run from C$65 for two,
including breakfast served
beside the stained glass window
in the dining room. Children and
pets are not accepted.

Restaurants

Dining at the Gingerbread
House is by prior arrangement
only, but the delicatessen at
Miner's Bay, the shops on Mayne
Street and the Trading Post pack
picnic lunches. (The nearby
service station rents bicycles
and most of the Mayne Island
roads are asphalted.) Or enjoy
fish and chips on the terrace of
Springwater Lodge, British
Columbia's oldest continuously
operating hotel; children are
welcome.
For dinner, try the medieval
meal at the rustic **Fernhill Lodge**,
(tel: 539-2544) which serves
hedgehogs in golden sauce,
partridge in Burgundy and
mushrooms, black porray, tart
for an ember day, herb salad,
flower cheesecake and cider
syllabub.

THE SUNSHINE COAST

The Sunshine Coast, a maze of
inlets, sheltered bays, verdant
forests and snow-capped peaks,
stretches 90 miles (150km) along
the Strait of Georgia, northwest
of Vancouver. The area claims
14 days more of sunshine a year
than Victoria, which is generally
regarded as the hot spot of
Canada. Rainfall on the Sunshine
Coast averages about 40 inches
(100cm) a year.
To get there, drive 30 minutes
northwest from Vancouver city
centre to the picturesque village
of Horseshoe Bay, known mostly
for fishing, boating and pubbing.
From there, BC Ferries make
eight sailings daily across Howe
Sound to Langdale. The breezy
open top deck of the ship, which
carries 360 vehicles and 1,400
passengers, affords a panoramic
view of nearby wilderness
islands. From Langdale, a two-
mile (3km) road winds west
through forests and farmland
along the craggy coast to
Gibsons, a vibrant village of
3,000 people. Known as the
Portal to the Sunshine Coast,
Gibsons is home to many retired
people and Vancouver
commuters, and is also home to a
popular television sitcom, *The
Beachcombers*. Visitors can tour
Molly's Reach, the set where the
show is filmed. Other options
include a harbour cruise around
the 400-boat marina and nearby
Keates island; a half-hour stroll
along the beach walk (lit at
night) to a stone cairn which
marks the spot where Captain
Vancouver landed 200 years
ago; poking into quaint shops
along the main street; seeing the
Salish Indian displays and 25,000
seashells at the Elphinstone
Pioneer Museum, and joining a
salmon fishing charter so that
you can carry home a coho or
chinook as a souvenir. West of
Gibsons, just off the main road,
are beautiful beaches, hiking
trails and picnic sites. Both

The ferry from Horseshoe Bay travels past beautiful wilderness

Roberts Creek, a community of artists and artisans, and **Porpoise Bay** sport clean and spacious campgrounds right on the water. About nine miles (14km) north of Gibsons stands **Sechelt** (population 5,000), the cultural and commercial heart of the Sunshine Coast. Scuba divers love the surrounding waters for the colourful and abundant submarine life. People who prefer to see seafood on a plate head for the Wharf Restaurant (on Davis Bay) and the Blue Heron, where solitary herons often stalk the shallow, marshy waters outside.

The Sechelt Indian Band office offers information about Canada's first self-governing Indian band, towering totem poles and, if you're lucky, a meeting with Mary, the oldest band member, who sometimes spends the day weaving cedar baskets in the old-fashioned way.

At **Egmont**, a four-hour rapids cruise provides a close look at the Skookumchuk ('strong waters') Narrows, where tides from three inlets rush at speeds of up to 16 knots through a rock-strewn passage. The winter and summer solstices have the highest tides.

Another ferry connects Earl's Cove with **Saltery Bay** across Jervis Inlet, with nine sailings a day in summer. Watch for pods of killer whales and playful seals who at times inhabit the inlet, along with the bald eagles overhead who live by diving for slow salmon. Anchored 60 feet (20m) down in Saltry Bay is a larger-than-life bronze mermaid who sometimes surprises scuba divers.

About 13 miles (20km) beyond Saltery Bay is **Powell River** (population 15,000), popular with anglers, moochers, trollers and buzz bombers who like really fresh blueback, chinook and coho for dinner. A large pulp and paper mill, which produced Western Canada's first roll of newsprint in 1912, supports the town. A little further along is **Desolation Sound**, popular with Canadian and American pleasure craft. This sound is the site of British Columbia's largest marine park. The warm waters and rich sea life, from little luminescent dinoflagellates to giant octopus, attract many divers.

To complete the circle tour back to Vancouver—which will take a few days—catch the ferry from Powell River to Comox on Vancouver Island (four sailings daily). Then drive down the coast to Nanaimo, where the ferry leaves for Horseshoe Bay. Or drive to Victoria and take the Swartz Bay ferry, which passes through the Gulf

Islands back to Tsawwassen.

Accommodation

The **Driftwood Inn** (tel: 885-7038, or toll-free from Vancouver 681-6168) is a comfortable place to stay, and also serves savoury seafood along with a great view of Vancouver Island. Historic Rockwood Lodge, nestled in a garden of giant sequoia, monkey puzzles, windmill palms and rhododendrons, is a community centre for arts, culture, recreation and education. North of Sechelt, the winding road roams past secluded Buccaneer Bay and Smuggler Cove. Lord Jim's Resort Hotel at Halfmoon Bay, features rustic verandahed cabins overlooking Malaspina Strait. Lord Jim fishing charters guarantee a catch.

VANCOUVER ISLAND

Islands conjure up all kinds of fanciful illusions. Mention Mallorca, Corfu, Cuba, Jersey, Tahiti or Fiji and the imagination turns to golden sands and sun; mention Vancouver Island, which stretches 280 miles (450km) along Canada's Pacific coast, and other images emerge: mossy, dense and dark rainforests of fir, cedar and hemlock; the wind- and surf-swept barren beaches of the Pacific; and, in Victoria, colourful baskets of flowers hanging from Edwardian lamp posts, and elegant afternoon teas.

The province should probably be called Columbia, because the region is no longer predominantly British, as people of many nationalities from around the world continue to flock here to live. But **Victoria**, which began as a Hudson's Bay Trading Post

in 1843, could well be called
British Victoria, because this
provincial capital retains some of
the best elements of British life.
Never mind that the provincial
Ministry of Tourism claims to
have no information of the city;
that the hostess at the city's
most popular seafood restaurant
insists that 'wharf' is spelled
'warf'; or that the maze from the
lobby to the underground
parking lot of the city's premier
hotel is as challenging as any
rainforest trail. People tend to be
more relaxed and forgiving on
islands. And the sun shines 50
per cent more here than in
Vancouver, a mere 60 miles
(100km) north.

*At night the grey stone of Victoria's
Parliament Buildings is transformed
by shimmering lights*

EXCURSIONS FROM VANCOUVER

The stately **Parliament Buildings**, sculpted in grey stone, dominate the Inner Harbour. Hourly guided tours show off the intricate stained glass windows, Italian marble panels, mosaic tile

Tour buses proclaim the British connection by the Empress Hotel

floors and painted murals illustrating the past of the province.

The nearby **Royal BC Museum**, at 675 Belleville Street, houses detailed displays of the province's past: a woolly mammoth, cobblestone streets bordered by turn-of-the-century shops, a working gold rush water wheel, a replica of Captain George Vancouver's ship *Discovery*, and mysterious masks and totems of the native Indians (open 09.30–19.00 hrs May to September and 10.00–17.00 hrs October to April; closed Christmas Day and New Year's Day). Next door is the **Helmcken House** house, built in 1852, which lends insight into the

life of a pioneer physician 140 years ago (open Wednesday to Saturday, 10.00–15.45 hrs). And adjacent **Thunderbird Park** has an outdoor display of replicas of old totem poles and original contemporary poles. The little **Emily Carr Gallery**, at 1107 Wharf Street, houses a representative collection of the artist's rainforest works and writings (open 10.00–17.00 hrs Monday to Saturday in summer and 10.00–16.30 hrs Tuesday to Saturday in winter).

Victoria has a good variety of shops and galleries, many selling British china and woollens, and antiques. Canadian native prints and carvings and the warm Cowichan sweaters hand-knitted in the Cowichan Valley north of Victoria are popular with visitors. The **Northern Passage**, at 1020 Government Street, houses distinctively Canadian crafts within an elegantly restored Victorian heritage building; items vary from fine pottery and silver jewellery to fluffy little abstract sheep which play Brahms' lullaby when patted on the back. It's worth browsing for a while at **Munro's Book Store**, at 1108 Government Street, just to see the magnificent domed ceiling, stained glass windows and wall hangings.

For an unusual morning, call **Artworld** (tel: 384-3766), where you can make your own watercolour souvenir sketch of this scenic city. Or call **Rent A Roadster** (tel: 361-7300) to drive a 1929 Model A Ford reproduction complete with rumbleseat around the city. You could also take a harbour cruise,

Colour has invaded the old quarry in Butchart Gardens' sunken garden

go fishing or spend a day at the **All Fun Waterslides** (open summer only) on Millstream Road (a 15-minute drive from the city centre). For information on other attractions and activities, visit the Travel InfoCentre at 812 Wharf Street (tel: 382-2127). About 13 miles (21km) north of Victoria are the **Butchart Gardens** (tel: 652-5256), quite possibly the most spectacular floral arrangement on the continent, which began as an abandoned limestone quarry in 1904. Meandering paved pathways lead through 50 acres (20 hectares) of exquisite living arrangements of more than 5,000 varieties of trees, shrubs and flowers. There is a sunken garden, a rose garden, a Japanese garden, an Italian garden, a star pond, a concert lawn, a fireworks basin and two restaurants and a coffee bar. In December, after the cornucopia of colourful blossoms has faded, ribbons of light brighten the grey days of winter. July and August see such added entertainment as musical reviews, puppet shows and fireworks. Wheelchairs, cameras, baby pushchairs and umbrellas are available (open daily from 09.00 hrs; closes at

23.00 hrs in July and August, around dusk in other months). An hour's drive north on Highway No 1 lies the little coastal town of **Chemainus**. About a decade ago, when the century-old sawmill closed and the town lay dying, a dream was born. A few artists began drawing larger-than-life murals on the exterior walls of buildings; the word spread, and other artists joined in. Today the town boasts Canada's largest outdoor art gallery, with 24 murals depicting the history of the Chemainus Valley. Subjects vary from a 19th-century brigantine to Hong Hing's grocery store and

Off-the-wall art in Chemainus

portraits of native Indians. There are several antique shops, art galleries, boutiques selling local crafts and souvenirs, and ice-cream parlours. The annual Festival of Murals in July features painters and sculptors at work, puppeteers, dramatists, street dances and parades.

Two miles (3km) south of Nanaimo, right on the edge of the roadway from Victoria, is tiny **Petroglyph Park**. If you blink, you might miss it. A short stroll through the woods leads to a series of Indian rock carvings, probably made with stone tools thousands of years ago: people, birds, bottomfish, and the mythical seawolf are represented and tableaux describe the findings.

Nanaimo, known as the 'Bathtub Capital of the World' for the annual race across Georgia Strait mid-July, is also famous for its 'bars'. The bars are rich layers of chocolate on top, butter and icing sugar in the centre, and a mixture of graham crackers and coconut and more chocolate on the bottom. From Namaimo, ferries run almost hourly back to the mainland at Horseshoe Bay. The next stop north should be **Campbell River**, self-proclaimed 'Salmon Capital of the World'. Thousands of anglers from around the globe congregate here every year, mostly from May to October. Many of the chinook caught are tyee class (more than 30 pounds or 13.6kg). Numerous fishing charters are available; or simply dangle a rod from Canada's first saltwater fishing pier, built here in 1987; rod and tackle rentals and bait available. Scuba diving is also a popular pastime because the strong tides produce an abundance of colourful marine life. For information on the dozens of lodges and motels in the area, visit the Travel InfoCentre (tel: 286-0764) in the museum.

An hour's drive west from Campbell River, **Strathcona Provincial Park** (tel: 284-3931) is another good spot for an outdoor holiday. The 580,000 acres (230,000 hectares) of wilderness include challenging peaks, alpine meadows, forests, lakes and Della Falls (Canada's highest) which cascade down 1,450 feet (440m). Strathcona Park is also home to the province's tallest Douglas fir (now celebrating its first millennium), which stands more than 300 feet (93m) tall.

No trip to Vancouver Island is complete without a visit to **Pacific Rim National Park**, on the western and rainy side of the island. Annual rainfall averages 120 inches (300cm); call 726-4212 for the weather forecast. Solitary beachcombers love Long Beach, a broad seven-mile (11km) stretch of surf-swept sand and tidal pools. A visit to the nearby

Weather permitting, you can explore Long Beach in perfect solitude

Wickaninnish Centre (tel: 726-7333; open daily, summer only) lends insight into the sometimes harsh haven that is the blue Pacific. Sightings of killer, humpback, finback, sperm and right whales are not uncommon in offshore waters; whale-watching cruises (March to October) are popular and often include seals, sea lions and bald eagles at no extra charge. Hardy hikers like the **West Coast Trail**, which meanders 48 miles (77km) along an old telegraph route through the wilderness rainforest, along sandstone cliffs and across slippery boardwalks; accessible May to October only.

Accommodation

Accommodation in Victoria varies. The recently-restored 480-room **Empress Hotel**, at 721

Government Street (tel: 384-8111), built in 1908, reigns downtown. The bed-time chocolates come with a weather forecast for the morrow. People who can't afford to stay here often stop for an elegant and gracious afternoon tea (four seatings daily; reservations recommended). Best Western's **Carlton Plaza** (tel: 1-800-663-7241 toll-free) is also within walking distance of Inner Harbour attractions. But the best accommodation bargain may be the **Victoria Youth Hostel** at 516 Yates Street, downtown (tel: 385-4511). To get to know the Victorians, call **Garden City Bed and Breakfast** (tel: 479-9999), who arrange accommodation in the local homes.

A half-hour drive north from Chemainus, on the Yellow Point Road, are the rustic **Yellow Point Lodge** (tel: 245-7422) and the luxurious **Inn of the Sea Resort** (tel: 245-2211), both offering waterfront accommodation. The Yellow Point Lodge does not accept children under 16 years. In Strathcona, **Strathcona Park Lodge** (tel: 286-2008), well-known for its wilderness programmes, offers reasonably-priced meals and accommodation in timbered waterfront cottages, apartments and campsites.

Restaurants

Good places to eat in Victoria include **Chandler's** (tel: 386-3232), identified by the big whale mural on an outside wall, which C-FAX 1070 AM Radio listeners voted the best seafood restaurant in the city. The **San Remo**, at 2709 Quadra Street (tel: 384-5255), which serves Italian and Greek food in a comfortable setting, is a favourite with reporters at the *Times-Colonist* newspaper; reservations not accepted, so be prepared for a wait, but it's worth it; food and service are excellent.

The **Bengal Lounge**, in the Empress Hotel (tel: 384-8111), serves a delicious curry, in a setting of re-created colonial splendour; a Bengal tiger guards the fireplace and the tapestry of textures includes heavy lace curtains, oriental rugs, rattan chairs, brass and porcelain safari-motif pots of tropical plants, fans hanging from an ornately carved wooded ceiling and a lushly canopied bar. **Rattenbury's**, in the Crystal Garden (tel: 381-1333), named in honour of Victoria's *fin-de-siècle* architect, specializes in grilled salmon marinated in pesto sauce.

Locals love **Spinnaker's Brew Pub**, at 308 Catherine Street in Vic West overlooking the Inner Harbour (tel: 386-BREW); the atmosphere is comfortably informal: self-service, terracotta floors with oriental carpets, twin dart boards, historical photos of Victoria past on the walls, a good pianist and outdoor waterfront tables in summer. The halibut and chips with Caesar salad is a favourite meal; in-house brews include Spinnaker Ale, Highland Scottish Ale and Empress Stout. For dessert, pick up some chocolate creams or almond brittle from **Rogers**, at 913 Government Street (tel: 384-7021), famous for fine candy for more than a century. More than

20 places serve afternoon tea; locals favour **Arthur's**, at 765 Fort Street (tel: 383-2850; 'reservations appreciated'), where the cost is considerably less. The friendliest place in Chemainus for lunch, although the cuisine is not *cordon bleu*, is **Mandolino's**, beside the railcar caboose InfoCentre (tel: 246-3231).

In Nanaimo, try a Mexican meal at **Gina's** (tel: 753-5411; reservations not accepted), perched on a clifftop across from the law courts. Gina's business card says 'A Tacky But Friendly Place'; the restaurant is friendly, the food tasty and the clientele interesting. If you miss mealtime in Nanaimo, drive north an hour to the **Old House** (tel: 338-5406; reservations advised) at Courtenay in the Comox Valley. Built in 1938 by a local pioneering family, the Old House features such island specialities as duck, pheasant, quail, oysters, salmon and rabbit. Although the restaurant is expensive, food and service are excellent.

WHISTLER/BLACKCOMB

Whistler/Blackcomb is becoming a subject for superlatives all over the world. North America's 50 million skiers recently rated this region second only to Vail, Colorado, as their favourite destination on the continent. Japanese skiers have named Whistler/Blackcomb the best ski resort in the world,

The World Cup ski run hurtles down towards Whistler Village

leaving Chamonix and Zermatt in the shadows. And *Snow Country* magazine gave it their top award for design excellence.

Whistler Village is 75 miles (125km) north of Vancouver on the Sea to Sky Highway. Sea to Sky is not an exaggeration. From the jagged coastline fringing Howe Sound to the west, the terrain rises quickly to dense rainforests and sheer rock faces with rushing waterfalls, up to alpine meadows flowering with Indian paintbrushes and lupin in summer and cloaked with snow in winter. Good mid-way stops *en route* are **Shannon Falls** just south of Squamish and the **BC Mining Museum** (tel: 688-8735) in Britannia Beach, once the largest copper producer in the British Empire and now a National Historic Site (open 10.00–17.00 hrs, Wednesday to Sunday mid-May to June, and daily in July and August; also weekends in September). Since this winding road can be especially hazardous during spring run-off and rains, some people prefer to travel with Maverick Coach Lines (tel: 255-1171), or BC Rail (tel: 984-5246), which leaves the North Vancouver station early each morning and returns mid-evening.

Whistler Village nestles at the base of the twin mountains of Whistler and Blackcomb in the Coastal Range. This village is a cluster of hotels, condominiums, shops and restaurants, most of them recently built in West Coast/European style. From the village square, it's a five-minute walk to the ski lifts, which service the two longest vertical drops on the continent: Whistler,

at 5,000 feet (1,525m) and Blackcomb, at 5,280 feet (1,609m). A 10-person express gondola whisks skiers up to the Whistler Roundhouse in 18 minutes, while two high-speed quad chair lifts run up to Blackcomb's Rendezvous Ridge in 20 minutes. About 25 per cent of the 200 downhill runs are designed for novices, about 55 per cent for intermediate skiers and another 25 per cent are tailored to experts.

After the warm spring sun has melted away the snows of winter, skiing on the Horstman Glacier takes over. During June and July intrepid glacier skiers share the lifts with mountain bikers, who ride down the same trails, now barren gravel, that alpine skiers slalom in winter; bikes are hung on the quad lifts. Summer brings golfers to the 18-hole Arnold Palmer championship course.

But recreation does not stop here. Hiking, horseback riding, canoeing, kayaking, river rafting, windsurfing and fishing in alpine lakes are also popular. More passive pursuits include sitting in the pavement cafés and watching the world go by.

Accommodation

Accommodation ranges from the inexpensive youth hostel at **Alta Lake** (tel: 932-5492) and the **KOA Kampground** (tel: 932-5181) to the 300-room **Delta Mountain Inn** (tel: 932-1982), with an outdoor heated swimming pool and jacuzzis, and the lavish new 350-room **Château Whistler** (tel: 938-8000), the largest château-style property built in Canada in a hundred years.

BRITISH COLUMBIA

'British Columbia ... if I had known what it was like, I wouldn't have been content with a mere visit. I'd have been born here.' Canadian humourist Stephen Leacock, 1937. Although still regarded as a youngster in the world community, British Columbia began when an upheaval in the earth created mountains here 130 million years ago. The first residents were Asian hunters and berry gatherers, who drifted south along the Pacific coast and into the interior around 6,000BC. The first visitor to arrive by sea was probably a Chinese Buddhist priest, 1,500 years ago; nowadays Asians are flocking to Canada's Pacific Province, both as tourists and immigrants.

A dazzling patchwork of eternal snow graces the Rockies

While Balboa claimed the Pacific Ocean and all its shores for Spain in 1513, Spaniards did not settle here until the late 18th century. They stayed only a few years, but left their names behind: Cardero, Valdez, Juan de Fuca, Bodega y Quadra and Malespina. Explorations by Captain Cook, Alexander Mackenzie, George Vancouver and Simon Fraser resulted in an influx of British settlers, and the area was declared a British Crown Colony in 1858. The province is now home to three million people, mostly clustered in the southwest. The quest for game, furs, gold, timber, land, oil and other resources created British Columbia, but tourism is now the number one industry. Most of the millions of visitors who come here each year are looking for wilderness. The province's 370,000 square miles (950,000 sqkm) is largely

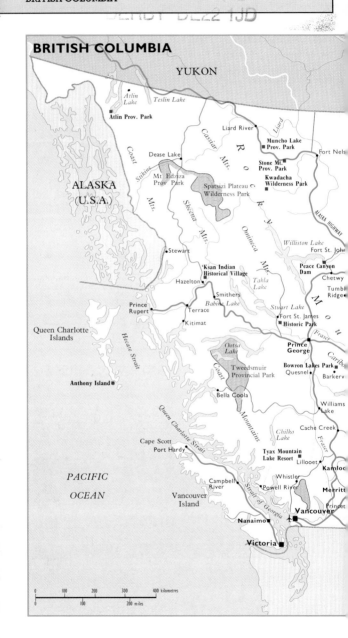

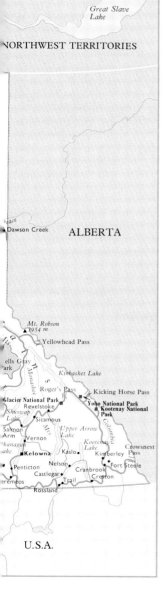

wilderness: a diversity of solitary beaches and quiet coves, primeval rainforest, spectacular fiords, snow-capped sierras, glacial lakes, pristine waterfalls, thermal springs, verdant valleys, arid desert and 6,500 islands scattered along the 7,500-mile (12,000km)-long coastline. What nature created, man has complemented with networks of highways and railroads, the largest fleet of ferries in the world, and numerous airports and seaplane bases. The hundreds of parks are deliberately undeveloped. In other regions man has constructed almost every conceivable recreation facility. The results are remarkable. British Columbia is a complexity of cultures. And for the most part, the wilderness remains wilderness.

WHAT TO SEE

BRITISH COLUMBIA ROCKIES

This region of scenic splendour stretches northwest from the 49th parallel along the Alberta border. Closed in by the lofty and eternal snows of mountains east and west, the main highway follows the Columbia River through the Rocky Mountain Trench, a broad valley of Ponderosa pine and Douglas fir. Archaeological findings suggest that the Kootenay Indians have lived here for 9,000 years. As hunters and gatherers, they knew all the secret passes through the mountains. When explorer and fur trader David Thompson eventually struggled through Howes Pass in 1807, the Kootenays nicknamed him 'Star

Clear waters and skies at Kicking Horse Pass in Yoho National Park

Man', because he seemed superhuman. Although explorers and traders, along with prospectors, missionaries and homesteaders followed, few settled. The discovery of gold at Wild Horse Creek in 1863 brought a surge of 5,000 souls, but when the gold was gone only about 20 families remained. While pioneers sought passes through The Rockies and prospectors pursued precious metals, most modern travellers head here in passionate pursuit of outdoor action. The air is fresh, the waters are clear and the sky is big. **Mount Assiniboine**, the Matterhorn of Canada, is a breath-taking 11,000-foot (3,600m)-high tusk of layered rock carved into a pyramid shape by glacial cirques. In **Kootenay National Park**, a half-hour hike through moss-carpeted forest leads to the Paint Pots, ponds stained red, orange and yellow by iron oxide, which the Kootenays used for body and rock painting. The Hoodoo Valley in Yoho National Park (see below), is home to wondrous and strangely shaped shafts of glacial silt and clay. Mining, forestry and tourism support the local economy. From such guest ranches as Top of the World, Beaverfoot and Bull River, visitors can canter around the countryside all day and return to find freshly caught rainbow trout sizzling on the grill. Others may prefer to hike over alpine meadows, paddle, sail, windsurf and waterski on emerald lakes. Or simply savour the silvery cascades of Laughing Falls, or soak in warmer water at the Radium, Fairmont or Lussier Hotsprings. Golfers find the spectacular scenery sometimes results in a golf game well above par. Wildlife watchers may spot moose, deer, elk, mountain goat, bear, lynx, coyote and marmots. Winter resorts offer nordic and alpine skiing, and heli-skiing in the Bugaboos of the Purcell Range is thrilling.

Fort Steele, 10 miles (16 km) northeast of Cranbrook, was abandoned at the height of its affluence as a gold-mining town at the turn of the century. The past is vividly present in the 50 restored buildings. Highlights include stagecoach rides, re-created old newspapers, Victorian vaudeville in the Wild Horse Theatre, and workers costumed as blacksmiths, carpenters, quilters, weavers, and a steam train (open all year round).

Kimberley, Canada's highest city, at 3,500 feet (1,117m), is called the 'Bavarian City of the Rockies'. The red-brick pedestrian plaza known as the Platzl holds the world's largest operating cuckoo clock. European delicatessens and restaurants serve such German specialities as *weisswurst*, *spetzle*, *sauerbraten* and *strudel*. In winter the town comes alive with skiers.

Yoho National Park is located just west of the Continental Divide and Banff National Park (tel: 343-6324). *Yoho* is an exclamation of wonder in the Kootenay language: an appropriate name for 28 peaks more than 10,000 feet (3,000m) high, all layered with rock, blue ice and snow. Sights to see here on the roof of the Rockies include Takakkaw Falls, the spiral railway tunnels which lead up to Kicking Horse Pass, and the Burgess shale fossil beds dating back 530 million years. Activities include horseback riding, canoeing and kayaking (motor boats not permitted), fishing, hiking, climbing and camping winter and summer (open all year round).

Rocky Mountain Visitors Association, PO Box 10, Kimberley, V1A 2Y5 (tel: 427-4838).

CARIBOO–CHILCOTIN

The untamed Cariboo–Chilcotin stretches almost right across the province, from the fiords of the Pacific to the forested foothills of the Cariboo Mountains in the east. The region evokes images of ranches of rolling hills and twisted lodgepole pine fences, with cowboys wearing ten-gallon hats roaming the range on frisky horses, quiet emerald lakes filled with kokanee, rainbows and Dolly Varden, gold-rush ghost towns and grizzly bears, and pioneer settlers still dreaming of independence and isolation. The main towns of **Williams Lake** and **Quesnel** (pronounced *kwuh-nel*) are on the banks of the mighty Fraser River. **Bella Coola** heads a rainforest fiord in the Valley of the Thunderbird, named after the mythological feathered friend of the coastal Indians, believed to be responsible for creating thunder, lightning and rain.

Europeans first came to this region 200 years ago. Explorer Alexander Mackenzie arrived overland from the east and Captain George Vancouver sailed into Bella Coola the same year, 1793. The Hudson's Bay Company established a trading post here in 1869. But a decade earlier, rumours of gold in the region had reached San Francisco and other points south. And a mass migration of prospectors, merchants and other gamblers followed the Cariboo Trail north from Lillooet to Barkerville, where as much as 675 ounces of gold was extracted in one day. Within five years the area produced C$40 million worth of the precious metal. But shortly thereafter the gold veins faded, and prosperity and people disappeared. Instead of boom towns, only ghost towns remained.

Barkerville, an hour's drive east from Quesnel at the end of Highway 26, is named after Billy Barker, a deserter from a British merchant ship, who found gold here in the 1860s. Barkerville became a ghost town a few years later when the gold ran out. More than 40 buildings dating from 1869 to the turn of the century were restored in 1958 and the town is now a historic site. A bakery (with great bread!), a photography studio, a mining shaft, a print shop, the Wake Up Jake Café, a blacksmith shop, St Savior's Church and the Theatre Royal bring alive the days of the Gold Rush: even boardwalks line the streets (open all year; no admission charge).

Bowron Lakes, a 90-minute drive east from Quesnel, is a chain of six major wilderness lakes and short portages, creating one of the best canoeing circuits in the country. Canoe rentals are available from June to September. For a nine-day escorted canoe tour, contact Pathway Tours, 5915 West Boulevard, Vancouver BC V6M 2X1 (tel: 263-1476). Cost includes guides, canoes, paddles, life jackets, tents, sleeping pads, safety gear, meals, accommodation and canoeing instruction.

The Hills Guest Ranch, in cooperation with 108 Resort and the Red Coach Inn, maintains 120 miles (200km) of nordic ski trails. The annual Cariboo Marathon attracts 2,000 skiers each February. The Hills is open all year round.

Tyax Mountain Lake Resort, a one and a half hour drive west from Lillooet, is sited amid Ponderosa pine and Douglas Fir along Tyaughton Lake, which means 'lake of the jumping fish' in the Chilcotin Indian language. The main lodge, the largest log structure in the province, features a native stone fireplace with bread-baking ovens built in. Available activities include horseback riding, fishing, boating, hiking, tennis, fossil-hunting and rockhounding and,

in winter, cross-country skiing, heli-skiing, snowmobiling, skating and ice fishing.
Cariboo Tourist Association, PO Box 4900, Williams Lake, V20 2VB (tel: 392-2226).

HIGH COUNTRY

High Country offers a lake a day as long as you stay: if you stay more than a year, you may have to start again; but the myriad lakes in this region offer so many amusements, you won't mind. **Sicamous**, the houseboat capital of Canada, is home to 310 miles (500km) of interconnected waterways through Shuswap Lake and Salmon Arm, and houseboating is a fine way to savour the scenery and maybe hook a few of the abundant kokanee, Dolly Varden or Kamloops trout for dinner. Apparently, salmon were once so plentiful here that local farmers speared them with pitchforks for fertilizer. Sailing, motorboating, swimming and windsurfing are popular pastimes today.

Water recreation is not limited to lakes. Try canoeing or kayaking through the gorge of the Adams River, cruising the reservoirs of the Columbia River or rafting the glacial green waters of the Thompson. Scramble over a sprawling glacier amid the passes and peaks of the rugged Canadian Rockies. Or watch sockeye salmon, the greatest navigators of all time, spawn in the Adams River. The thundering waterfalls at **Wells Gray Park** are breathtaking. And

Whether you cross it by foot or by air, the Fraser River is a fearsome sight at Hell's Gate

BRITISH COLUMBIA

the aerial tram at **Hell's Gate** on the Fraser River, lends an eagle's eye view of the churning waters below.

Other outdoor options include hiking over flowery alpine meadows or through dense forests of cedar, hemlock, fir, spruce and pine in the **Monashee Mountains**, or riding the range of semi-arid sagebrush and tumbleweed desert near **Kamloops**, sometimes called the 'Sunshine Capital'. When the mantle of winter moves in, alpine and nordic skiing and snowmobiling become popular.

What nature has provided, man has made accessible, although it has taken a couple of centuries. Nearly 200 years ago, when the hunting and fishing Shuswap Indians were the only residents, the Columbia River became a freeway for fur traders heading westward to the Pacific. Prospectors for gold rushed to the region north of Revelstoke in the 1860s, mostly via the Thompson River. A mule track followed the river in part and sternwheelers carried the gamblers across the lakes. About 200 overlanders, including a pregnant woman with three children, came by a horsecart from Quebec and walked across The Rockies through Yellowhead Pass. Most floated down the Fraser in dugout canoes or on log rafts, but 36 of them hiked to the head of the North Thompson and rafted downstream, and settled on Kamloops Lake.

After British Columbia became a province in 1871, the same routes were used to complete the cross-Canada railway. The last spike was driven at Craigellachie in 1885. At about the same time, the genteel Cornwall brothers established a cattle ranch at Ashcroft and relished such rituals as afternoon tea, after a hard day of riding through sagebrush and scrub with hounds at their heels in pursuit of coyotes. The most recently built road in the region is the classy Coquihalla Highway from Hope to Kamloops, which shortens the driving time to four hours.

Revelstoke is located at the western end of Roger's Pass, one of the world's most scenic routes. Grizzly Plaza, downtown, is backdropped by wooded hills and frosted mountains. But the best sights are seen from the road and the hiking trail to the summit of Mount Revelstoke. Helicopters whisk visitors summer and winter to the nearby Durrand Glacier. The Revelstoke Dam is one of the largest and most modern on the continent.

Roderick Haig-Brown Conservation Area, located 70 miles (110km) east of Kamloops, is the site of the largest sockeye salmon run on the continent. Every four years a million salmon (fewer in other years) find their way 300 miles (485km) upstream in 17 days in early October. It's shattering to watch their silver bodies turn red, as they spawn and then roll over and die, while bears on the banks and eagles overhead prepare for a feast.

High Country Tourism Association, PO Box 962, Kamloops, VC2 6H1 (tel: 372-7770).

Big cities have no place in Kootenay Country, where roads and rivers squeeze between plunging canyons

KOOTENAY COUNTRY

Kootenay Country nestles between the Rocky Mountains and the fertile rolling land of the Okanagan–Similkameen (see page 53) in southeastern British Columbia. Steep mountains separate narrow valleys of rivers and six long lakes, emerald in summer and frosty white in winter, leaving no room for big cities. The choppy terrain never permitted a successful railway, and there are no freeways here. The rivers, and subsequently the roads, twist north and south and east and west. The population of the three largest towns, Trail, Castlegar and Nelson, totals only 25,000. And Greenwood (population: 800) claims fame as Canada's smallest city.

Although Kootenay Indians have navigated the whimsical rivers of this region for centuries, and weathered a mini-ice age little more than 200 years ago, explorer David Thompson, who navigated most of the 1,200 miles (1,950km) of the Columbia River from source to sea early in the 19th century, was unable to find his way through that part of the river in Kootenay Country. Europeans and Asians arrived in the late 1800s for copper, gold, silver and lead. By 1897 the region was producing almost all Canada's silver and lode gold and, by World War I, all the copper for the British Empire. When the magic metals faded, most settlers left, but a few stayed. Trail, a sternwheeler post in the 1890s, is still home to Cominco, the largest lead and zinc smelting complex in the world. However, most of the ores are imported.

Rossland, which sits on the site of an extinct volcano, is sometimes called the 'Golden City', since more than a million dollars' worth of gold was extracted here. But prospectors have been replaced by skiers, who gambol on the famed powder snows. Creston, today a small tapestry of fields of seed and root crops, was once home to the unusual Kootenay canoe with bow and stern both under water. A similar canoe found in the southeastern Soviet Union suggests that Indians did migrate from Asia across the

Nelson is an important centre of Canada's artistic life

Bering Strait.

At **Kaslo**, the SS *Moyle*, last of the local sternwheelers, recalls a bygone era. It is now a museum dedicated to other sternwheelers (open daily 10.00–16.30 hrs, mid-April to mid-October). From the waterfront cafés in the picturesque fishing village of Balfour, you can watch or catch the longest free ferry ride on the continent—a half-hour journey across Kootenay Lake. There is half a mile (800m) of passages to explore at Cody Cove. Hardy hikers have acres of wilderness in Valhalla Park; adventurers can tackle the rapids, and canoers can enjoy the quiet ripple of paddles. Less energetic visitors may simply soak in the steaming hot springs, open all year round at Nakusp and Ainsworth.

Nelson, on the south shore of

Kootenay Lake, was formerly an iron and silver mining settlement, which turned to trees and logging when the mines were depleted. More than 300 Victorian buildings have been faithfully restored, including the city hall and the courthouse, designed by FM Rattenbury, also architect of Victoria's Provincial Parliament and the Empress Hotel. Nelson claims more artists and artisans per capita than any other place in Canada. The hilly, tree-lined streets, backdropped by superb ski mountains, were the setting for the 1987 movie *Roxanne*. The old-fashioned restaurant at the **Heritage Inn**, downtown, provides a pleasant meal.
The Doukhobor Historical Village, across from Castlegar airport, represents through buildings, artefacts and art a communal settlement of pacifist Russian immigrants who lived here from 1908 until the 1930s. The restaurant serves such traditional Doukhobor vegetarian fare as *borsht* and *perogies*, and a shop sells Doukhobor crafts. The 5,000 Doukhobors who still live in the area are still pacifists, and many still speak Russian. Nearby Zukenberg Island Park was the home of Russian Alexander Zukenberg who came here in 1931 to teach Doukhobor children (open daily, 08.00–20.00 hrs).
Kootenay Country Tourist Association, 610 Railway Street, Nelson, V1L 1H4 (tel: 352-6033).

NORTH BY NORTHWEST

North by Northwest encompasses one-third of British Columbia. It streches westward from the Rocky Mountains, across plateaux of dense coniferous forest, dotted with crystal lakes and mountain ranges hiding fast-flowing rivers, to the Queen Charlotte Islands in the Pacific Ocean. North is The Yukon, and to the south lies the Cariboo–Chilcotin. With the population hovering around 200,000, North by Northwest has a lot of space. In the remote Atlin/Dease Lake area, there is an average of 70 square miles (180 sq km) for each resident.
Prince George is the gateway to the region. Other towns include Prince Rupert, Terrace, Kitimat and Smithers. Landforms vary from 600,000-year-old Pre-Cambrian rocks to Canada's youngest lava beds, formed 250 years ago near Terrace. The native Carrier, Haida, Tlingit and Tsimshian Indians have roamed this region for 8,000 years. Russian, Spanish, British and American explorers arrived only 200 years ago. The Yellowhead/Tête Jaune Highway was named after a rare fair-haired Iroquois hunter, lured to the northwest by a fur trading company around that time. In 1806 Simon Fraser sailed two birchbark canoes to Stuart Lake, where the Carrier Indians believed tobacco smoke to be escaping spirits of dead ancestors. Here, Fraser built Fort St James as the capital of New Caledonia. After the explorers and fur traders, gold prospectors came and went, and homesteaders who preferred pine needles to pavement arrived to tame the wilderness—at least a little.

*A noble profile on a 'Ksan Historical
Indian Village totem*

Most have learned to live with
their fellow creatures: black
bear, grizzlies, coyotes, moose,
black-tailed deer, mule deer,
beaver, muskrat, marten,
porcupines and at higher
elevations mountain goats, sheep
and caribou. The coast is misty
and moody rainforest. Prince
Rupert locals say that in the
morning you first put on your
raincoat, then you look outside to
see what the weather's like. But
the most mystical rainforest is
the **Queen Charlotte Islands**,
sometimes known as 'Galapagos
North'. Although decimated by
smallpox and other diseases of
the white men, the native Haida
have managed to keep alive

some traditions, and have kept
so-called civilization at bay.
On Anthony Island in the Queen
Charlottes is **Ninstints**, the best
preserved totem village in the
world, which was declared a
UNESCO world heritage site in
1981. Weathered and brooding
Haida totems and remnants of
old long houses contrast with the
freshness of tall cedar forests
lush with mosses and giant ferns.
Permission to visit Ninstints must
be obtained from Haida chiefs.
'Ksan Historical Indian Village,
near Hazelton (tel: 842-5544), is a
reconstructed Gitksan village,
which includes community
houses for the Frog, Wolf and
Fireweed Clans, a smokehouse
for fish and meat, a burial house,
a food cache, a carving studio
and several magnificent totems.
An hourly guided tour relates
how Indians used to live, along
with their legends and beliefs
(open daily May to mid-October,
09.00–18.00 hrs).
Fort St James Historic Park (tel:
966-7191) evokes the flavour of a
19th-century Hudson's Bay
Company fur trading post. A
half-hour guided walking tour
includes a general warehouse,
complete with goods, a fur store,
a fish cache, a bachelors'
bunkhouse and a vegetable
garden (open daily May to
September, 10.00–18.00 hrs).
Spatsizi Plateau Wilderness Park,
between Smithers and Dease
Lake, encompasses 670,000 acres
(270,000 hectares) of primeval
wilderness, including a rolling
plateau and the glaciated Skeena
Mountains. Spatsizi means 'red
goat', for local goats take on a red
coat from their habit of rolling in
the iron oxide dust.

Hikers and boaters must share this back country with caribou, moose, mountain goats and grizzlies, as well as various smaller mammals and 140 species of birds, including gyrfalcons. Eight cabins, a cookhouse and a sauna at Cold Fish Lake are for public use.

Accommodation

Esther's Inn at 1151 Commercial Drive, Prince George (tel: 562-4131) is a mini Honolulu-North, worth a stop, if only for lunch poolside at the Papaya Grove Café. Loggers and miners love to come to town to relax at Esther's. Rooms are reasonably priced and the food is good. The rooms ring around a courtyard which resembles a tropical oasis and is filled with ferns, palms, philedendrons, waterfalls, jacuzzis and Polynesian artefacts.

North by Northwest Tourism Association, PO Box 1030, Smithers, V0J 2N0 (tel: 847-5227).

OKANAGAN–SIMILKAMEEN

This small, L-shaped region, which hugs the American border in south central British Columbia, comprises the Similkameen River Valley and the Okanagan Valley. The warm climate has made the region home to the highest concentration of people anywhere in the interior of the province. The sun shines about 150 days and precipitation averages 10 inches (25cm) each year. The main cities are Kelowna (population: 60,000), Penticton (population: 30,000), and Vernon (population: 20,000). Although fur traders were here 150 years ago, and gold

Okanagan–Similkameen is a particularly fruitful region

prospectors began panning the streams and creeks shortly thereafter, serious settlement started with Oblate priest Father Charles Pandosy, who meandered in on horseback in 1859, and found arable land. Thanks to him, the region now produces all the marketable apricots in Canada, along with 60 per cent of the cherries, 50 per cent of the pears and plums, 30 per cent of the apples and 20 per cent of the peaches.

This land of peaches and beaches attracts hordes of Canadian and other visitors in summer. Springtime (in April and May) sparkles with beautiful and fragrant blossoms and

BRITISH COLUMBIA

The blue expanse of Okanagan Lake stretches into the distance

autumn sparkles with wine, as a dozen wineries flourish here. Winter visitors enjoy alpine skiing at Big White Mountain near Kelowna, Silver Star near Vernon and Apex Alpine near Penticton, which means 'place to stay forever' in the language of the nomadic Salish Indians. The Similkameen Valley boasts four dozen trout lakes, and there may be as many hues of green and blue in Kalamalka Lake. California bighorn sheep graze in winter and spring on the high cliffs shadowing Vaseux Lake which harbours largemouth bass, rainbow trout and carp. Ice fishing is also a possibility. Okanagan Lake, which stretches 90 miles (144km) north to south, claims seven provincial parks, Canada's longest floating bridge and the legendary Ogopogo, a sea serpent believed by some to have been hatched from a

wayward dinosaur egg, belatedly released by a movement in the earth's crust. Recreation in the region varies from a soothing mineral massage at Cedar Springs and waterplay at half a dozen waterslide parks, to cruising aboard the paddlewheeler MV *Fintry Queen* and rockhounding for jasper, agate and opal in the sagebrush above Keremeos. The **Federal Ecological Reserve**, a 'pocket desert' located just south of Oliver, is the northern extension of the American Great Basin Desert, which runs south to Mexico. Although irrigation has turned much of the arid land of the Okanagan into fertile orchards and vineyards, the antelope bush, sage, rabbitbrush and prickly pear cacti of the pocket deserts provide a habitat for burrowing owls, turkey vultures, spadefoot toads, coyotes (which the Indians call God's dogs), kangaroo rats, with their fur-lined external pockets for carrying seeds, and shy northern Pacific rattlesnakes. Black-headed grosbeaks, American redstarts, northern orioles, Lewis' woodpeckers, chuckar partridge and kestrels also call this desert home.

The **O'Keefe Ranch**, on Highway 97, was established in 1867 on the grassy rolling hills near the northern tip of Okanagan Lake. Visitors enjoy the original log home, a working blacksmith shop, St Ann's Catholic Church, which held its first mass in 1889, the O'Keefe Mansion, luxuriously furnished with *fin-de-siècle* antiques, the Chinese cook's bunkhouse and a fully-stocked general store (open daily, 09.00–17.00 hrs, mid-May to early October, extended to 19.00 hrs in July and August).

The **Father Pandosy Mission** was built in 1859 on the outskirts of present-day Kelowna to serve both native Indians and white settlers. The mission, which comprises log buildings, a chapel and a schoolhouse, all restored to illustrate pioneer life, is an official heritage site.

Okanagan Similkameen Tourist Association, 515 Highway 97 South, Kelowna V1Z 3J2 (tel: 769-5959).

PEACE RIVER ALASKA HIGHWAY

This serene valley is cradled by the foothills of the Rocky Mountains to the west and the vast Alberta prairie to the east.

Rivers of the region flow east and north to the Arctic Ocean. Nature and time have transformed the once lush subtropical valley, where dinosaurs dined on flowering plants and evergreen forests, to oil and gas. The re-routing of part of the Peace River during dam construction unearthed footprints 100 million years old. Two centuries ago, explorers and traders Alexander Mackenzie, John Finlay, David Thompson and Simon Fraser greeted Sekani, Beaver and Carrier Indians here. And in spite of one gold-rush in the 1860s and another 40 years later, it was the 1,500-mile (2,450km)-long Alaska Highway, built in nine months in 1942 by 27,000 Canadian and American workers, that really opened up the region. The highway is not a straight one. Legend says that a soldier, sent out on snowshoes to survey the route near Fort Nelson, found the walking rough, so he followed a moose who created an easy trail. The bulldozers faithfully followed, plotting every twist and turn. The highway, which is mostly hard-surfaced and is open all year round, begins at **Dawson Creek**, known as Mile Zero, a popular summer recreation area for camping, hiking, swimming, canoeing and fishing. There is alpine skiing in winter at nearby Bear Mountain.

Fort St John, 47 miles (75km) up the highway, was once a fur trading post, but today is known as the 'Land of the New Totems', after the tall oil derricks silhouetted on the horizon. Lumbering and sheep and cattle ranching also contribute to the economy. **Tumbler Ridge** is an interesting town in that it was created practically overnight seven years ago to mine coal. The fertile black soil of the **Peace River Valley**, along with the long summer days, nourish good crops of wheat and canola, which is used to make linseed oil. Wild berries thrive; late summer sports abundant supplies of wild strawberries, blueberries, raspberries and low-bush cranberries. Where there are berries, there are usually bears. Approach dense bushes with caution, singing, shouting, yodelling or whistling all the while, and the bears generally retreat. Observant travellers may also see coyote, wolf, lynx, moose, stone sheep, porcupine, beaver, red-throated loons, peregrine falcons, golden eagles and great-horned owls. Magenta fireweed, wild roses, purple lupin, violets, columbines, heather and lilies compose a cornucopia of colour against the big sky. And thanks to great fields of clover and 35,000 beehives, 4.5 million pounds (2 million kg) of honey are produced each year. But the beauty is not limited to daylight hours. In late autumn and early spring, the Northern Lights dance across the night sky.

Liard River Hot Springs, located 125 miles (200km) from The Yukon border, has an unusual microclimate, with 80 species of plants (including eight carnivorous ones) not found anywhere else in the province. A rustic boardwalk meanders through a jungle of monkey flowers, ostrich fern, loelia and

orchids to dozens of pools, some adapted for swimming. Although the water smells like sulphur, the temperature is 114°F (45°C).

The Peace Canyon Dam, located 4¹/₂ miles (7km) from Hudson's Hope, on Highway 29 at the outlet of the Peace River Canyon, re-uses water that has already generated electricity further upstream at the Bennett Dam. The Visitors' Centre has two models of duck-billed dinosaurs that inhabited this region during the Mesozoic Era (open daily from 08.00–17.00 hrs Victoria Day to Thanksgiving Day; Monday to Friday 08.00–16.00 hrs in winter; closed holidays).

Peace River Alaska Highway Tourist Association, Box 6850, Fort St John, V1J 4J3 (tel: 785-2544).

PEACE AND QUIET

Wildlife and Countryside in Vancouver and British Columbia
by Paul Sterry

Canada is a country of stunning beauty. Vast tracts of unspoilt wilderness offer fabulous opportunities for naturalists and anyone wanting to enjoy the great outdoors. Set on Canada's Pacific coast, British Columbia has everything from temperate rainforests and mighty rivers to tranquil alpine lakes and snow-capped peaks. Although the region certainly merits lengthy tours away from towns and cities, many wonderful areas can easily be reached on one-day outings from Vancouver itself.

Travel a short distance inland from Vancouver and you reach

Man is humbled by nature in Canada: Vancouver Island's Cathedral Grove

alpine meadows and icy mountain summits which are home to forest birds and black bears. A ferry journey across the Strait of Georgia takes you to immense Vancouver Island, whose western side is flanked by rainforest. Plant life abounds in the damp climate, and sealions and whales abound in the seas.

In and Around Vancouver

Vancouver has a reputation for being one of the cleanest and most attractive modern cities in the world. The pride that British Columbians take in their urban environment is reflected in the surprising variety of wildlife that still thrives within the city's

PEACE AND QUIET

boundaries. Almost any area of greenery or open water will hold interesting plants, mammals and birds, but recreational parks and wildlife refuges within Vancouver offer the best opportunities for the visiting naturalist. Stanley Park, which juts out into Burrard Inlet, is a well-known recreational area with a mixture of natural and altered habitats including woodland, parkland, freshwater lakes and shoreline. Numerous song birds, such as Wilson's warblers, orange-crowned warblers, eastern kingbirds, as well as downy and

In many parks, black bears are indifferent to human visitors

pileated woodpeckers and rufous hummingbirds, can be found among the park's trees. Many of Stanley Park's resident birds, and mammals too, are accustomed to the presence of man and some will even come to food. Wildfowl gather on Beaver Lake and Lost Lagoon, while around the seashore, bald eagles, ospreys, great blue herons, pigeon guillemots, scoters and Brandt's cormorants can be seen.

The George C Reifel Bird Sanctuary lies in the mouth of the Fraser River on Westham Island and is a wonderful refuge for water-loving birds. Wintering wildfowl such as brent geese, Canada geese, snow geese and American wigeon are particularly impressive, but many species, such as cinnamon teal and wood duck, are also present during the breeding season. A collection of tame birds enables visitors to get good views of otherwise wary species.

Migrant waders (or shorebirds) are also abundant during spring and autumn migration. Among the more frequently encountered species are western sandpipers, least sandpipers, greater yellowlegs, lesser yellowlegs, semi-palmated plovers, whimbrels and short-billed dowitchers. Great blue herons, green herons and American bitterns are often seen stalking through shallow water in search of fish.

Cypress Provincial Park

Lying a short distance to the north of Vancouver and bordered on the west by Howe Sound, Cypress Provincial Park affords spectacular views back over the city and on to Vancouver Island and the Gulf Islands. Cross-country and downhill skiing opportunities are good in the park but for those who simply want to walk and enjoy the scenery and wildlife, the network of well-maintained trails and paths of varying lengths caters for all abilities and interests.

Access to the park is via the Cypress Parkway, which winds its way north from Routes 1 and 99. From the parking area, it is a comparatively short walk to Yew Lake along the Interpretive Trail, while routes such as the Baden Powell Trail and the Howe Sound Crest Trail will take you further afield and should not be attempted alone or by the inexperienced or unfit. Leaflets are available which can help plan a circular route.

Within the park's boundaries, the forests are dominated by coniferous trees such as Douglas fir, western hemlock, amabilis fir and yellow cypress. The latter two trees are very slow growing and only thrive in the moist climate of coastal British Columbia. Botanical variety is supplied by brilliant white sprays of western flowering dogwood as well as by alders and vine maples. The latter species is thought to derive its name from its often twisted and gnarled appearance. Ferns and mosses grow in abundance in glades and forest clearings, alongside skunk cabbage, huckleberry and marsh marigold.

The birdlife of Cypress Provincial Park is typical of forests in western British Columbia. Varied thrushes and hermit thrushes feed on the forest floor while chestnut-backed chickadees, red-breasted nuthatches, crossbills, gray jays and a variety of warblers and flycatchers can be found foraging among the branches.

The park's mammals include gray squirrels, chipmunks and black bears. Visitors would do

PEACE AND QUIET

well to heed the warnings of the park authorities who suggest keeping all items of food securely locked in the boot of your car. The bears have become fearless of man but should under no circumstances be fed. Such enticement may lead to a bear becoming a nuisance or a danger, with the result that it may have to be destroyed—a sad and unnecessary consequence of thoughtless feeding.

Mount Seymour Provincial Park

Along with Cypress Provincial Park, Mount Seymour is a favourite recreation destination for Vancouver's inhabitants. In winter, there are good skiing facilities while in summer, trails and paths allow extensive exploration of this wonderful wilderness area. Day-visitors can make use of the picnic areas set in scenic positions, while for those wanting a longer stay, designated campsites are available and wilderness camping is permitted in some of the more remote regions. Three dramatic peaks lie within the park's boundaries: Mt Bishop, 4,946 feet (1,508m), Mt Elsay, 4,653 feet (1,418m) and Mt Seymour, 4,766 feet (1,453m). Not surprisingly, the scenery is spectacular and views throughout the park stretch as far, weather permitting, as the Gulf Islands and Vancouver Island. The best views of all are had by using the Mystery Peak chairlift, a year-round facility which takes visitors to the summit of the mountain. As with nearby Cypress Provincial Park, the forests comprise mainly coniferous trees such as western hemlock, Douglas fir and western red cedar, with amabilis fir, yellow cedar and mountain hemlock predominating towards the snow-line. An excellent network of trails winds through the park and visitors should have no trouble planning a circular route to suit their interests, experience and fitness. The Flower Lake loop trail and the Goldie Lake loop trail are particularly rewarding, with the latter doubling as a self-guided nature trail.

The birdlife of the park makes good use of the abundant fruits, berries and seeds. Crossbills prise seeds from pine cones, while cedar waxwings and blue grouse prefer berries. Resident chestnut-backed chickadees, pine siskins and red-breasted nuthatches have a more mixed diet which includes insects; summer visitors such as Hutton's vireos and willow flycatchers feed more exclusively on invertebrates.

The park's mammals include squirrels and chipmunks as well as larger creatures such as coyotes, mule deer and cougar. These latter species are somewhat wary of man and, although they are occasionally seen from cars, are more likely to be encountered in remote parts of the park. This aversion to man is not shared by all Mount Seymour's mammals—black bears are sometimes seen extremely well.

Golden Ears Provincial Park

The stunning scenery of Golden Ears Provincial Park lies only

30 miles (50km) or so east of Vancouver. The drive from the city is easy and access to the park is through the town of Haney, just north of the Fraser River. Dominated by the Coast Mountain Range, the northern border of Golden Ears adjoins Garibaldi Provincial Park and the two areas have much in common: awesome, snow-capped mountain ranges, extensive forests and beautiful lakes. The unusual name of the park derives from the twin peaks of a mountain whose snow covering glows at sunset and is supposed to resemble a pair of ears.

From the southern entrance to the park, a road runs north along the shores of Alouette Lake. From here, numerous trails lead off into the mountains and forests and, as with most Canadian parks, excellent information leaflets and trail maps help visitors plan a route to suit their interests and capabilities. The Menzies Trail and Lower Falls Trail are comparatively short, while the Golden Ears Trail and the Alouette Mountain Hiking Trail are for more experienced walkers.

From the shores of Alouette Lake, wildfowl such as Barrow's goldeneyes, ring-necked ducks and bufflehead can be seen with many other species occurring from time to time. Spotted sandpipers and the occasional heron or American bittern feed around the lake margins and beavers sometimes ripple the water's surface as they swim. Streams and rivers throughout the park are the haunt of belted kingfishers, American dippers and harlequin ducks, with the

An industrious rodent: the beaver modifies its environment by felling trees and damming rivers

latter two species often being found in the most turbulent water.

From the shores of the lake, forests of western red cedar, Douglas fir, birch, red alder and maple give way to yellow cedar, alpine fir and mountain hemlock at higher elevations. Lowland forest glades are rich in flowers that attract insects such as swallowtail and Camberwell beauty butterflies as well as rufous hummingbirds. The birdlife includes American robins, cedar waxwings, Steller's

PEACE AND QUIET

jays, crossbills, ruffed grouse and numerous warblers and flycatchers, while the forests are also home to squirrels, mule deer and wapiti (elk).

Against all odds, salmon ascend rivers from the sea to spawn

Garibaldi Provincial Park
The park derives its rather unusual name from the 8,860 feet (2,700m) Mount Garibaldi, which is volcanic in origin and was itself named in honour of the famous Italian revolutionary. Garibaldi Provincial Park is a comparatively short drive north of Vancouver and is reached via designated access points on Highway 99, which runs along its western edge. Thereafter, this vast wilderness area has to be explored using one of the park's trails, but visitors benefit from the vast amount of work that the park's authorities put into maintaining this network.
The five most popular access points are, from south to north, Diamond Head, Black Tusk,

Cheakamus Lake, Singing Pass and Wedgemount Lake. Throughout the park there are vistas of forests, alpine meadows, lakes, waterfalls and snow-capped mountains. The circular routes from Diamond Head and Black Tusk (the latter in the vicinity of Garibaldi Lake) are perhaps most rewarding. During the summer months, the alpine meadows are a riot of colour with the beautiful yellow flowers of arnica growing alongside small clumps of grass of Parnassus, lilies, anemones, Indian paintbrushes and lupins. Marmots have their burrows in these meadows and keep a wary look-out for predators. If a golden eagle or red-tailed hawk is spotted soaring overhead, they whistle in alarm. The park's other mammal residents include mountain goats, mule deer, and both grizzly and black bears. At high altitudes, the forested slopes of Garibaldi Provincial Park comprise hardy tree species such as mountain fir and yellow cedar. Lower down, western red cedar, Douglas fir and western hemlock predominate, interspersed with patches of cottonwood and birch beneath which a ground flora of ferns, mosses, salmonberry and huckleberry can be found. Several species of warblers and flycatchers forage among the branches during the summer months and woodpeckers and red-breasted nuthatches search crevices in the bark for insects. The waters of Daisy Lake, Garibaldi Lake and Cheakamus Lake are worth watching for wildfowl which may include bufflehead, Barrow's goldeneye and blue-winged teal as well as harlequin ducks outside the breeding season.

Manning Provincial Park

Manning Provincial Park lies over 125 miles (200km) east of Vancouver, but few visitors are disappointed after having made the effort to get there. Access is comparatively easy since Highway 3 cuts through the heart of the park *en route* from Hope to Princeton. The mountains are undeniably dramatic and form a perfect backdrop for the beautiful forests, alpine meadows, lakes and rivers which make up the rest of the park. As with British Columbia's other parks, an excellent system of trails, paths and campsites, used in conjunction with information leaflets and the Outdoor Recreation Council of British

Columbia's Maps 8 and 11, ensure that the scenery and wildlife can be enjoyed to the full. Three trails are of particular interest to the naturalist: the Rhododendron Flats Trail, from which flowering rhododendrons can be seen in June; the Beaver Pond Trail, which is the haunt of wildfowl such as blue-winged teal and cinnamon teal; and the Paintbrush Trail, which visits subalpine meadows, full of colourful flowers in the summer months.

The route of Highway 3 runs close to the Skagit and the Similkameen rivers during its passage through the park. Belted kingfishers perch on overhanging branches and are sometimes seen in flight, when they utter their characteristic rattling call. Spotted sandpipers and American dippers perch on riverside boulders, while over the forested slopes of the valleys, goshawks and Swainson's hawks rise on updraughts.

The forests are composed of a variety of trees such as Douglas fir, western hemlock, birch and cottonwood. Pileated woodpeckers, Clark's nutcrackers, red-breasted nuthatches, chestnut-backed chickadees, ruby-crowned kinglets and several species of warblers forage in the foliage and branches throughout the summer months, while among the ground vegetation, blue grouse feed unobtrusively. Areas of ponderosa pine and lodgepole pine, such as those found in the Skagit Valley Recreation Area, are more open woodland in which it is easier to birdwatch than in denser stands of conifers. The forests are also home to mammals such as chipmunks, squirrels, mule deer and black bears.

Pacific Rim National Park

Mention British Columbia to anyone who has not visited the region and images of alpine landscapes of mountains and snow and vast tracts of coniferous forest are conjured up. What could be more surprising, therefore, to discover that along the Pacific coast there are wonderful areas of rainforest? These are not the hot, steamy jungles of Central and South America but cooler, temperate rainforests with lush, evergreen trees festooned with lichens and mosses and a rich understorey of herbaceous plants. The Pacific Rim National Park, on the west coast of Vancouver Island, protects one of the finest areas, and excellent trails, information centres and leaflets help visitors get the most from a visit.

The Pacific Ocean, which provides the moisture that helps the forest thrive, also exerts a moderating influence on the climate. Snow and ice are the exception rather than the rule in winter and many plants can grow throughout the year. By contrast, the summer months are often cool, when fog or rain are frequent, if short-lived, features of the weather.

The landward fringes of the shoreline, which are strewn with driftwood, are colonised by wind-pruned and stunted trees. Here, sitka spruce predominates, while inland, western red cedar, Pacific silver fir, western yew and western hemlock are more common. Many of the trees in the rainforest are hundreds of years old and the decaying remains of fallen giants abound. The practice of leaving dead wood where it falls is essential to the survival of the forest: nutrients are returned to the soil by fungi and add to its fertility.

Beneath the tree canopy, berry-bearing shrubs and bushes such as huckleberry, blueberry, twinberry and salal grow in abundance. The forest floor is a carpet of fallen leaves and twigs, mosses and liverworts, and hosts a wealth of flowers such as twinflower, salmonberry, bunchberry, skunk cabbage, false lily of the valley and several species of orchid.

Birdlife is also rich in Pacific Rim National Park. Seabirds such as sooty shearwaters, pigeon guillemots, Brandt's cormorants and the occasional tufted puffin and rhinoceros auklet can be seen from the shores. The beaches themselves throng with migrant waders in spring and autumn. Semi-palmated plovers, surfbirds, wandering tattlers, least sandpipers and western sandpipers join resident black oystercatchers and variety is boosted by several species of gulls, wildfowl and herons. Migrating California gray whales are sometime seen from headlands during October and November and April and May. From the trails and paths in the rainforest, breeding woodland birds such as Townsend's warblers, Wilson's warblers, orange-crowned warblers, dark-eyed juncos, Swainson's thrush, golden-crowned kinglets, chestnut-backed chickadees, cedar waxwings, Steller's jays and band-tailed pigeons may be seen. Pileated woodpeckers and hairy woodpeckers investigate branches and trunks for insects, but most extraordinary of all is the sight of rufous hummingbirds searching the trails and clearings for nectar-bearing flowers.

Strathcona Provincial Park

Strathcona, which dominates the centre of Vancouver Island, is British Columbia's oldest provincial park. It is a region of rugged beauty with lakes, forests and alpine meadows set against a backdrop of snow-capped mountains and dramatic waterfalls. Within the Strathcona's boundaries, the park authorities have developed excellent facilities for visitors; campgrounds, hiking trails and nature trails are well set out and

Aptly named: bunchberry produces bright red berries in autumn

allow extensive exploration of the region. Cross-country skiing is permitted during the winter and, in summer, wilderness camping is allowed, provided that park regulations are observed. However, because of the nature of the terrain and the changeable weather, planning, safety and a realistic appreciation of your own capabilities are essential. Strathcona contains a mountain called the Golden Hinde which, at 7,200 feet (2,200m) is Vancouver Island's highest peak. Despite the elevation of this peak, and indeed much of the park itself, the climate is comparatively mild thanks to the moderating influence of the Pacific Ocean. Alpine meadows are found between the permanent snow-line and the tree-line and support beautiful cushions of moss campion (moss catchfly), carpet phlox, alpine paintbrush and many others. The higher forested slopes support stands of mountain hemlock and

PEACE AND QUIET

juniper while lower down, Douglas fir, western red cedar, western hemlock and amabilis fir predominate. Glades, rides, forest edges and the banks of streams support a rich understorey of mosses, lichens and ferns.

Lakes, ponds and marshes are a feature of many upland areas of the park, particularly the Forbidden Plateau, but the

Harlequins are elegant ducks that frequent whitewater torrents

immense Buttle Lake and the contiguous Upper Campbell Lake dominate the centre of the Strathcona. Belted kingfishers, geese and ducks, such as Barrow's goldeneye, mallard and bufflehead, are found around the shores of the lake while the forested slopes rising from the water's edge are home to blue grouse, ruffed grouse, Steller's jays, gray jays, chestnut-backed chickadees, red-breasted nuthatches and a wonderful variety of birds of prey and owls.

Woodland mammals are less varied than in mainland parks, mainly due to the offshore isolation of Vancouver Island,

which has reduced colonisation. However, mule deer (black-tailed deer), wapiti (elk) and wolves are all present although rather difficult to see.

USA National Parks

Olympic National Park is relatively easy to reach either by road from Vancouver or by ferry from Victoria to Port Angeles in Washington State. Dominated by the snow-capped Olympic Mountains, the western side of the park has extensive temperate rainforests, while to the east, in the rainshadow of the mountains, forests of western hemlock, western red cedar, dogwood and red alder predominate, with colourful alpine meadows being found above the tree-line.

Blue grouse, American robins, hermit thrushes and ground squirrels feed on the forest floor; Steller's jays, Townsend's warblers, ruby-crowned kinglets and many other species forage in the trees above. Vaux's swifts hawk for insects over the tree-tops and golden eagles soar overhead for hours on end. Dominated by the Cascades Mountains, North Cascades National Park lies 125 miles (200km) east of Vancouver. It lies just over the national border to the south of Manning Provincial Park in British Columbia and its scenery and wildlife bear a strong resemblance to its Canadian neighbour.

Victoria

British Columbia's capital, Victoria, lies at the southeastern tip of Vancouver Island. The opportunities for visitors with an interest in natural history are

The wapiti or elk stands up to five feet (1.5 m) tall: a magnificent sight in a forest clearing

excellent and the city is especially good for birdwatching. Victoria's parks host a wide variety of resident and migrant woodland birds and the shores and coastal waters have waders, wildfowl, gulls and auks in abundance.
Birdwatchers from Europe will also be intrigued to hear skylarks in song-flight over fields close to the city, these birds having been introduced earlier this century.
Clover Point is a favoured coastal birdwatching spot where, depending on the time of year, black oystercatchers, black turnstone, wandering tattlers and surfbirds can frequently be seen.
Offshore, marbled murrelets, guillemots, harlequin ducks, scoters, divers, grebes and gulls are often abundant during the winter months, peaking in numbers in late autumn and early spring. Ferry crossings to

Port Angeles and Seattle are good for sea birds such as sooty shearwaters and skuas and groups (called 'pods') of killer whales are often seen.

Whale Watching and Sea Birds
British Columbia offers almost unrivalled opportunities for naturalists wishing to observe sea birds alongside the ocean's most spectacular inhabitants—whales. Boat trips operate out of many harbours, but it is not always necessary to make special trips in order to see these beautiful creatures; sightings of whales as well as sea birds are often made from ferry crossings or dry land.
The west coast of Vancouver Island, and in particular the Long Beach area of the Pacific Rim National Park, is the best place

PEACE AND QUIET

to see California gray whales. These friendly giants migrate north to Alaska to feed during the summer months, making the return trip each year to their calving lagoons on the Pacific coast of Baja California in Mexico. The journey north takes them past British Columbia from March to May with the return passage occurring during October and November. Almost any headland along Long Beach may be good and some have telescopes in position to assist viewing. The Whale Centre (tel: 725-3163) operates zodiac whale-watching trips to see the grey whales on the west coast. British Columbia is perhaps even more famous for its killer whale population which inhabits the calmer waters between Vancouver Island and the

A humpback whale: one of many species of cetaceans seen off the coast of British Columbia

mainland. Ferry crossings between Vancouver, Victoria (on Vancouver Island) and Washington State frequently produce sightings and whales are sometimes seen from the Gulf Islands. However, the narrow Johnstone Strait is generally considered to be the best place to see them. Stubbs Island Charters (tel: 928-3185) offers daily trips between June and September from Telegraph Cove, and Biological Journeys, based in California (tel: (707) 839-0178), operates longer trips both to Johnstone Strait and to other whale hot-spots through British Columbia's Inside Passage to Alaska. These trips also offer chances to see Steller's sealions and harbour seals. During whale-watching trips and ferry crossings, other species of cetacean such as Dall's porpoise or humpback whale are occasionally seen together with a variety of sea birds.

FOOD AND DRINK

According to American Express, Vancouver has more restaurants per capita than any other place in North America. Those that are good are often very good and some that are bad are horrid. Only good ones will be mentioned here, and good does not necessarily mean expensive. The great variety of cuisines, varying from bannock and oolichans to bagels and osso bucco, is a reflection of the city's past and present. Dinner usually costs a few dollars more than lunch for the same menu and breakfast is the bargain of the day. Many restaurants are closed on Monday, and it's best to phone ahead. Reservations are recommended for lunch during the week and for dinner Friday and Saturday evenings. Most restaurants accept most credit cards. Restaurants do not add in a service charge, so some waiters and waitresses rely on tips for a respectable income. Although Canadians sometimes tip as much as 20 per cent, there's no need to tip if food or service is substandard.

Breakfast and Brunches

The **Westin Bayshore Garden Restaurant and Lounge**, at 1601 West Georgia Street (tel: 682-3377), serves a great Sunday brunch. While the views of Coal Harbour, Stanley Park and the North Shore mountains are spectacular, the buffet which spills out into the lobby is also a feast for the eyes. There are carts of fresh and candied fruit, cereals and nuts, while artistic sculptures in lard decorate tables of meats, eggs, pastas and salads. Omelettes are prepared to order. A selection of breads and cheeses clusters around a central fountain. The sweet-toothed may favour the maple crêpes served from the *à la carte* menu. Dress is casual or elegant. The price is about C$17 for adults and, for children, a dollar for every year of the child's age (up to age 12); children age four and under are free.

Dim Sum, which means 'a little bit of heart' in Cantonese, is a popular breakfast and lunch served every day of the week in Chinatown and in Chinese restaurants throughout the city. Dim sum regulars arrive early and sit near the kitchen for first choice of the freshest food from the procession of little carts carrying dozens of delicacies. Favourites include **ha gow**, a thin rice dough wrapped around bits of prawn and bamboo shoots steamed; **cha siu bao**, dumpling-like buns filled with barbecued pork and lemon and egg tarts. Dim sum diners can eat a little or a lot and pay accordingly. The green jasmine tea, robust black bo lei, served at no charge, goes well with the dim sum, as does local or Chinese beer. Good dim sum restaurants include the **Flamingo**, at 3469 Fraser Street (tel: 877-1231), the **Pink Pearl**, at 1132 East Hastings Street (tel: 253-4316), and **Ming's**, at 147 East Pender Street (tel: 683-4722) in Chinatown. For take-out dim sum, stop at **Maxim's Bakery**, at 257 Keefer Street (tel: 688-6281), two blocks away.

The **Alma Street Café**, at 2505 Alma Street (tel: 222-2244), serves breakfast in a mellower mood, with classical piano and

FOOD AND DRINK

harp as background for Sunday brunch. Large potted plants, an aromatic mountain of breads and pastries and good paintings by local artists decorate the restaurant. The menu includes everything from omelettes to scrambled tofu with eggplant and spinach, carrot juice and cappuccino, and a wonderful West Coast salad of sorrel, chickweed, purselane, pansies and pea blossoms. Skip the pecan pie for dessert and the total adds up to about C$15 per person.

For a quaint cultural experience, visit the **Elbow Room Café**, at 720 Jervis Street (tel: 685-3628). Hopefully, the bulldozers will be kept at bay. The little place is plastered with newspaper clippings and publicity photos of such past customers as Tom Selleck, Raymond Burr and Robert Redford. Although there are only half-a-dozen tiny tables, the eatery vibrates with the energy of the two owners, who are also the chefs, who are also the waiters, and who exort you to finish your pancakes and to answer the phone because they don't have time. Breakfast is served all day until closing time at 15.30 hrs.

Joe's, at 1150 Commercial Drive (phone number unlisted), creates one of the best cappuccinos in the country. While punks play pool, local radicals, feminists, philosophers and Kitsilano yuppies watch television and attempt to solve the problems of the universe. For a quiet cappuccino in a more sophisticated setting, try **Café Milieu**, at 1145 Robson Street (tel: 684-4600), which bakes the best

brioches and croissants to be found in the city.

Fast Food

Delicatessens at Granville Island and Robson Street Markets and on Commercial Drive sell great varieties of cold meats, cheeses and ready-made salads. **Troll's**, at several locations (tel: 689-9140), is famous for fish and chips. But **Fresgo's**, at 1138 Davie Street (tel: 689-1332), fills up famished teenagers with bacon and eggs and hamburgers and French fries for the least amount of money. And numerous **White Spots**, **Wendy's** and **McDonalds** serve thousands of burgers from restaurants scattered throughout the city. Most food markets and shopping malls house a cluster of fast-food outlets which serve everthing from sushi to souvlaki.

Other Restaurants

African: The inexpensive **Kilimanjaro**, at 332 Water Street (tel: 681-9913), is one of the great undiscovered treasures in town. While savouring cucumber soup, samosas, baked trout with tamarind and mango, and yams, you can watch shoppers and sightseers watching the steam clock of Gastown. Request a window table.

Canadian Indian: The **Quilicum**, at 1724 Davie Street (tel: 681-7044), is a simulated Indian longhouse of poles and beams, gravelled walkways and sunken tables, with colourful native masks (for sale) decorating the walls and recorded Haida folk songs as background music. The chef works over an open grill on an alderwood fire, which sometimes becomes a little smoky. Specialities include caribou, barbecued goat ribs, salmon cheeks, wild rice and whipped soap berries (Indian ice cream).

Chinese: Dozens of Cantonese and Szechuan restaurants dot Vancouver, especially in Chinatown. If the clientele is mostly Chinese, you can be sure the food is good. The **Won More**, at 1184 Denman Street (tel: 688-8856), serves a spicy but inexpensive Szechuan dinner, with a view of the sunset over English Bay; cash only. At the other end of the economic scale, the **Tai Chi Hin**, at 888 Burrard Street (tel: 682-1888), serves more than 200 dishes, including fresh rock cod, smoked fried duck, and green beans with chilli peppers. If you order a Chinese banquet, the lobster's little eyes are lighted red with batteries hidden inside.

East Indian: Although food critic James Barber likes the **Ashiana** at 5076 Victoria Drive (tel: 321-5620) best, visitors may prefer the **India Gate**, located downtown at 616 Robson Street (tel: 684-4617).

It is certainly well worth a visit for fans of East Indian food, as the curries are inexpensive and delicious. A good tip for those on a budget.

French: **Le Crocodile**, at 818 Thurlow Street (tel: 669-4298), may be the least expensive good French restaurant in town. But the **Café de Paris**, at 751 Denman Street (tel: 687-1418), which resembles a classy bistro on the Left Bank, is exceptionally comfortable. The service is consistently good, and the food is always excellent.

You can eat Indian food and buy Indian masks at The Quilicum

Greek: Across the Lion's Gate Bridge in West Vancouver is **The Greek Connection**, at 1560 Marine Drive (tel: 926-4228). It's worth the drive; or else take the blue bus from Georgia Street across for dinner. Although some people liked it better as a greasy little hole-in-the-wall, the modernized décor still recalls those romantic little Greek islands. For a light and inexpensive meal, combine the spinach pie in phyllo pastry with a Greek salad and pitta bread.

Italian: Although excellent Italian restaurants checker the city, you can always rely on **Umberto's** five restaurants. The service is superior (except perhaps in

FOOD AND DRINK

Settebello) and the food is fine.
Il Giardino, at 1382 Hornby
Street (tel: 669-2422), takes the
cake with its Tuscan villa décor,
complete with a terracotta tiled
courtyard for summer al fresco
dining. The antipastas, pastas,
Caesar salad and especially the
calamari and mussels are
delicious. Expect to pay about
C\$30 for a three-course lunch
with a glass of cabernet.
Japanese: Many of the 40
Japanese restaurants in town can
be pricey, but **Kamei Sushi**, at
811 Thurlow Street (tel: 684-
4823), and four other locations
are both reasonable and
reliable. Menu items vary from a
portion of salmon sushi for a
couple of dollars to the Love Boat
Dinner, which includes miso
soup, sunomono salad, rice,
teriyaki, gyoza, fried chicken,
prawn tempura, yakitori, orange
sherbet and green tea for a very
reasonable price—all served in
a picturesque little sailboat. The
box lunches (eat in or take out)
are also a bargain.
Korean: Dinner at **The Korean
Gardens**, at 845 East Hastings
Street (tel: 255-5022), is an
inexpensive cultural experience.
The waitress brings a tray of
meats and vegetables, chopped
into bite-sized bits, to your tatami
room, and you cook dinner
yourself over little gas grills. Be
careful with the side dishes of
kimchee (pickled cabbage),
which can be a trifle spicy for
western palates.
Mexican: Although **Pepita's**, at
1170 Robson Street (tel: 669-
4736), is lively and well-located,
it's worth the 10-minute hike to
the little **El Mariachi Restaurant**,
at 735 Denman Street

(tel: 683-4982), if only for the
superior chocolate chicken and
thirst-quenching margaritas.
Prices are reasonable at both
places.
Spanish: El Patio, at 891 Cambie
Street (tel: 681-9149), and **La
Bodega**, at 1277 Howe Street (tel:
684-8814), share the same owner,
and Spanish dining informality
and conviviality prevails at both
restaurants. La Bodega is the
closest place to Spain on this
continent. The best meal is a
series of tapas (appetisers)
shared among several people.
Choose from zesty potatoes,
garlic fried chicken (which, if
marketed on the same scale,
might put Colonel Sanders out of
business), stewed
Mediterranean vegetables,
sizzling prawns and sausages
only a European could make.
The prices at La Bodega are
pretty reasonable. La Bodega is
much more crowded in the
evening than at lunchtime.
Vietnamese: Vina Restaurant, at
851 Denman Street and at other
locations around the city (tel:
688-3232), is one of the few
places to fill up a strapping 16-
year-old for less than C\$10. The
combination plate, which
includes fried Vietnamese rolls,
crêpes, brochettes and rice,
satisfies both gourmets and
gourmands. Service is excellent.
West Coast: Delilah's, hidden
underneath the Buchan Hotel at
1906 Haro Street (tel: 687-3424),
offers a set-price two-course and
a five-course dinner. From the
old railroad-style menu you
check off desired dishes,
including such local specialities
as wild mushroom soup,
gathered greens salad, pheasant

pâté and grilled salmon. The **Raintree**, at 1630 Alberni Street (tel: 688-5570), is the queen of creative West Coast cuisine. The menu features sorrel soup, fish chowders, wild greens with edible flowers, braised salmon and the mile-high Okanagan apple pie topped with a slice of Cheddar cheese. Wide windows and ample space between tables add to the northwest ambience.

View Restaurants

Canadian author Bruce Hutchison says; 'The history of Canada for about 300 years was a struggle to escape from the wilderness, and for the last half century has been a desperate attempt to escape into it.' Vancouverites love their local scenery and many visitors come especially to see it. While a good view sometimes means mediocre food, the following restaurants offer both spectacular scenery (when the sun is shining) and good food.

Rebecca's apple pie tempts the tastebuds at The Raintree

The Beachside, at 1362 Marine Drive in West Vancouver (tel: 925-1945), lets you watch windsurfers and sailing boats tacking around freighters in English Bay on a summer day. Be sure to request an outside table, for inside you see nothing. Reasonable.

The classic **English Bay Café**, at the corner of Denman Street and Beach Avenue (tel: 669-2225), is a crowded but fine site to catch a summer sunset. Reasonable.

At **Seasons**, in Queen Elizabeth Park (tel: 874-8008), a foreground of flowers is backdropped by scenic water and mountains. Lamb is the most popular item on the menu, but the steamed mussels Nishino are also tasty. Reasonable.

The **Sundowner** (tel: 921-8161), open May to October only, is nestled between steep wooded hills and the water's edge on Howe Sound, a 10-minute drive

FOOD AND DRINK

north of Horseshoe Bay. The calamari and Caesar salad make a great meal. Terrace tables provide a great view of a playful and hungry harbour seal and a little flotilla of ducks who navigate among the fishing boats and yachts. Reasonable.

The cheerful and cosy **Teahouse**, at Ferguson Point in Stanley Park (tel: 669-3281), has an idyllic verdant setting, even when rain showers the glass roof of the adjacent conservatory. Reasonable.

Vistas, which revolves atop Stanley Ho's New World Harbourside Hotel at 1133 West Hastings Street (tel: 689-9211), provides a dramatic panorama of the city and harbour. Expensive.

Where to Drink

Although most people come to Vancouver for the scenery, an occasional aperitif has been known to enhance a sunset. Drinking as a pastime has been falling out of favour. Southern Europeans, known for their love of the fruit of the vine, have long advised that alcoholic drinks should be accompanied by tapas, antipastas or meses. The trend now in North America is to combine drinking with a meal, or at least a snack. In Vancouver there are many pubs, bars and lounges to while away the hours. The **George V**, in the Georgia Hotel, and the **Elephant & Castle**, in Pacific Centre, both downtown, are fairly typical of British pubs. The deck at **Stamp's Landing**, located on scenic False Creek, is a good spot to sip away a summer evening; residents, boat owners and singles hang out at this neighbourhood pub.

Farther afield at the **Mountain Shadow Pub**, at 7174 Barnet Highway in Burnaby, locals love playing darts, shooting pool and watching Monday night football. **The Troller's Pub**, in Horseshoe Bay, attracts a lot of locals for the superb jazz (15.00–18.00 hrs Saturday) and live rock and blues (Friday and Saturday evenings).

Hemingway would probably have liked the **Gerard Bar**, at Le Meridien Hotel, where pastoral paintings, tapestries, antlers and an elk's head decorate the dark but glossy maple walls; winged chairs and a gas fireplace add to the ambience. The **Garden Lounge**, in the Bayshore Hotel, replete with bamboo, rattan, tropical plants and a classical music trio in the evening, is reminiscent of Somerset Maugham's South Pacific; Trader Vic's bar in the same hotel is also popular. The **Garden Lounge** in the Four Seasons Hotel is a central place to meet, or retreat from the bustling shopping centre below. The airy **Cascades Lounge**, at the Pan Pacific Hotel, provides a panorama of Burrard Inlet and the mountains beyond. For years singles have been flocking to the **Pelican Bay** lounge in the Granville Island Hotel, and its popularity does not seem to diminish. The bar/lounges in the **Sylvia Hotel** and the **English Bay Café** are good places to watch the sun set. The **Arts Club** lounge on Granville Island is an interesting spot for an after-theatre drink. And the bar at **La Bodega** is a favourite with writers, editors and the advertising set.

SHOPPING

Vancouver has been a shopping centre for British Columbians since the Oppenheimer brothers began outfitting prospectors and other pioneers late in the last century. Forty years ago, West Vancouver's Park Royal, now housing 190 shops, opened as Canada's first major shopping centre.

The question today is not what to buy but where to begin. City stores cater for jet-set sophisticates, casual continental tastes, cheap souvenir seekers, urban and suburban workers, and geologists, lumbermen and homesteaders from the hinterland.

North American shopping malls have become the town squares and village fountains of the present day. Shopping has become a destination, a recreation, entertainment and, occasionally, a cultural activity. Teenagers like to hang out in malls and senior citizens often choose malls as a place to rendezvous. In sprawling suburbs, where the **Metrotown** centre, for example, holds parking for 3,500 cars and is linked to city centre by Skytrain and hundreds of buses daily, shopping has become a preferred pastime.

Some of Vancouver's spacious modern malls reflect the latest trends in architecture and design. Others are historical heritage sites restored to former grace and elegance. Colourful clusters of shops hug the water and street fronts in other areas. Most stores are open Monday to Saturday 09.30–18.00 hrs (with hours extended to 21.00 on Thursdays and Fridays) and

Variety is the spice of shopping and there's plenty on Robson Street

treats

Sunday 12.00–17.00 hrs.
Pacific Centre, downtown
beneath and north and south of
the Four Seasons Hotel, is a good
place to begin. The 200-store
complex boasts shopping sales
of C$100 million annually
(excluding Eatons). A three-
storey waterfall, a glass rotunda
and skylighted atrium almost
bring the outdoors indoors.
Eatons and The Bay department
stores cater to every taste; watch
for their sales—the bargains are
genuine. Eddie Bauer
specialises in sporting goods
and outdoor apparel. Holt
Renfrew, Brigitte, Monet, Cactus

*Pacific Centre, a glittering palace for
the Vancouver consumer*

and Mr Jax stock high fashion
designer names. Marks &
Spencer sells inexpensive
British wear, in contrast to the
costly adornments under glass at
nearby Cartier. The Den for Men
and Harry Rosen provide the
latest in masculine tailoring.
Bowrings and the Dower
Cottage sell assorted giftware.
The Body Shop, committed to
preserving the environment, and
Crabtree & Evelyn house
excellent collections of
fragrances, cosmetics and health

and beauty products.

Two blocks north towards Canada Place stands **Sinclair Centre**, a restored heritage building with elegant columns and marble stairways joining the two levels. Such shops as Leones, a galleria of exquisite European designer creations, complete with espresso bar, Gulliver's Travel Accessories, Blackberry Books and a dozen food outlets surround the central atrium, which is often decorated with exhibitions of good paintings. A short distance east from Sinclair Centre and Canada Place is **The Landing**, an award-winning heritage building, which hugs the harbour on the western fringe of Gastown and sports spectacular water and mountain views to the north, assuming the clouds are cooperating. Interior views are equally enticing. The Polo Country Store sells Ralph Lauren sportswear; the Quarterdeck has clothes, nautical charts and gifts for almost any kind of voyage; Super Shirts specialises in souvenir sweat shirts; the Edinburgh Tartan Shop sells warm woollens; and a series of other shops sells gifts and gadgets. A few doors east from The Landing, still on Water Street, where the cobblestones and imitation gas lamps recall pioneer days, is the **Inuit Gallery**, with Eskimo sculptures in stone and bone and colourful coastal Indian masks and other artefacts. Neighbouring **Heritage Canada** sells such Canadiana as Cowichan Indian sweaters, mukluks and moccasins. **Neto** stocks soft leathers in the latest European colours and styles,

along with complementary accessories. **Artemis Antiques**, at 321 Water Street, presents unusual and pricey treasures. Numerous other shops and restaurants line the streets of Gastown.

Six blocks south is **Robson Street**, where a casual stroll is a cosmopolitan adventure. This street is now the place to see and be seen in Vancouver. The Robson Street Fashion Park, a plaza of marble pillars capped with a cupola of arched glass, features such fashion celebrities as Alfred Sung, Ralph Lauren and Benetton. Next door are Club Monaco with casual clothes and Laura Ashley's romantic Victorian paisleys and floral prints. Nearby Villeroy & Boch, 'the talk of the table since 1748', offers an impractical-to-pack array of dinnerware, crystal and giftware. The rest of Robson Street is lined with boutiques featuring everything from fine fragrances and country collectables to remaindered books. **Duthie's** is the city's best known bookstore.

Various cafés and restaurants allow ardent shoppers to refuel before forging on.

Other downtown malls, such as **Royal Centre** and **Harbour Centre**, also house numerous shops. And exotic **Chinatown** is only a 10-minute walk away. Vancouver is home to more than 100,000 Chinese people, so Chinatown is abustle with stocks of rattan and bamboo ware, antique rosewood furniture, fine silk blouses and scarves, beaded sweaters, oriental art, jewellery and porcelain and a profusion of herbal remedies.

SHOPPING

The **CC Arts Centre**, at 20 East Pender Street, houses an interesting array of antique Chinese porcelain, delicate rice papers and artistic photography, and owner CC Lam enjoys talking politics if you want to chat for a while. In contrast, just across the street, the **KC Book Company** hawks such delightful trinkets as musical greetings cards with blinking coloured lights.

Granville Island, an urban park development with renovated warehouses turned into theatres, stores, art studios, restaurants and a popular food market, is a pleasant place, even on a rainy afternoon. The Circle Craft Shop stocks selected British Columbia arts and crafts. The Crystal Ark, tucked away near the colourful Creekhouse Gallery, sells natural rock crystals and gemstones from around the world. And there are bookstores and bakeries, delicatessens, the Kids' Only Market and the Granville Island Brewery.

In the **South Granville** shopping area, stretching roughly from 6th to 16th Avenue, antique collectors enjoy Uno Langmanns' 18th- and 19th-century furniture, oriental rugs and other *objets d'art*, as well as Portobello's store of 18th-century antiques, furniture, silver and pewter. Nearby Hampshire Antiques sells period British furniture. The Harrison and Bau-Xi galleries, Martha Sturdy's jewellery and several Persian carpet emporia share the same neighbourhood. And there is fine fashion at Mondo Uomo, Boboli, Byblos and Bacci's.

The **West Tenth Avenue** shopping scene, near the University of British Columbia, includes Kaboodles, with ultra-fantastic toys for kids of all ages; Panache, with handcrafted jugs, goblets and jewellery; Devonshire Antiques, with continental porcelain and unusual handcrafted furniture; Peasantries, which specialises in unique gifts from Quebec; Le Fil de Linges, with a line of linen both classic and contemporary; and Byron & Company's, with good buys in Thai, Turkish and Balinese goods.

The Oakridge Shopping Centre, at West 41st Avenue and Cambie Street, houses 150 stores, including Abercrombie & Fitch, Rodier Paris, Edward Chapman, Ports, Bally Shoes, Bowrings, the Salt Box and Woodward's department store, all set in a spacious skylighted mall, where a feeling of quiet sophistication prevails. Across Burrard Inlet, on North Vancouver's waterfront, is **Lonsdale Quay**, a food market full of fresh seafood and other tasty treats from around the world. The second level is devoted to retail stores carrying giftware and fashions. But the spectacular views of Vancouver's magnificent downtown skyline may deter even confirmed shopaholics for a while.

And remember **Park Royal** and **Metrotown**. As if these were not enough, **Sport Tours** (tel: 732-7622) offers shopping tours to West Edmonton Mall in sales-tax-free Alberta. Prices run from about C\$300 per person, including airfare, transfers and two nights' accommodation.

ACCOMMODATION

Vancouver and the rest of
British Columbia provide a
great selection of
accommodation, varying from
top-of-the-line view suites in
luxurious hotels to drive-to-your-
door motels, youth hostels,
campgrounds and bed and
breakfast in private homes.
Remember that room size and
quality may vary within one
establishment. Reservations are
recommended, The Infocentre
at Four Bentall Centre, 1055
Dunsmuir Street operates a
hotel reservation service (tel:
683-2772). The current hotel tax
is 10 per cent. Accommodation
listed here is either in or very
close to downtown Vancouver.
For further information, request
the comprehensive BC
Accommodations Guide from
your nearest Tourism Canada
office, or write to BC Tourism,
Parliament Buildings, Victoria.

*The 50-year-old Hotel Vancouver,
with its distinctive copper roof,
towers over Robson Square*

Deluxe Hotels
Canada has five hotels with a
CAA/AAA five-diamond rating.
Three of these, the Four Seasons,
Le Meridien and the Pan Pacific,
are in Vancouver. The city's
deluxe hotels almost all have
stunning mountain, water or city
views (request a view room
when you reserve), swimming
pools, saunas, spas, health clubs,
several restaurants and bars,
lobby shops, concierge, 24-hour
room service, valet parking and
conference rooms. Most hotels
are wheelchair accessible.
Some offer seniors' discounts,
family discounts, weekly
discounts, honeymoon
packages, and various off-season
rates.
Delta Place, 645 Howe Street
(tel: 687-1122). This elegant

ACCOMMODATION

property has 197 rooms, with fine furnishings. Views of Vancouver's spectacular mountains and waterways are limited.

Four Seasons, 791 West Georgia Street (tel: 689-9333). The Four Seasons is right in the heart of downtown and sits atop Pacific Centre, a subterranean mall comprising 200 shops. The hotel is modern, with elegant furnishings in all 385 rooms. Four Seasons Hotels are renowned throughout North America for superior service.

Hotel Vancouver, 900 West Georgia Street (tel: 684-3131). The Hotel Vancouver, which recently celebrated its 50th birthday, is the oldest deluxe hotel in the city. Its colourful copper roof has been a landmark to many world travellers, including such notables as King George VI and Queen Elizabeth. The 508 guest rooms include the four-bedroomed Royal Suite on the 14th floor, decorated in Renaissance style and featuring a fireplace, crystal chandeliers and a baby grand piano. Orchestra leader Dal Richards has entertained guests in the Rooftop Restaurant and Lounge for almost five decades.

Hyatt Regency, 655 Burrard Street (tel: 687-6543). With 646 units, the 34-storey Hyatt is the largest hotel in Vancouver. Rooms have superior residential furnishings and some have balconies. Underneath the building is Royal Centre, with numerous shops and 10 small cinemas. Hotel staff speak 32 languages. Two floors are reserved for Regency Club

members and feature keyed access, a private lounge, concierge service, complimentary breakfast and evening *hors d'oeuvres*. Camp Hyatt offers special activities and rates for children age 15 and under (see **Children**, page 93).

Le Meridien, 845 Burrard Street (tel: 682-5511). Le Meridien has 397 European-style rooms and suites and manages the adjacent La Grande Residence, comprising 162 spacious one- and two-bedroomed apartments (minimum stay one month). Gerard Restaurant features different regional specialities of France at different times of the year. The hotel's spa treatments range from eyebrow arching to 'a full day of beauty'. Chocoholics find the joy of chocolate in the two dozen items featured at the Chocoholic Bar on Friday and Saturday evenings.

New World Harbourside, 1133 West Hastings Street (tel: 689-9211). This hotel overlooks one of the busiest harbours on the continent and the North Shore mountains. If you have a room with a city view instead, dine at the revolving restaurant on top. If that makes you dizzy, retreat to the Dynasty Chinese restaurant off the lobby, seat yourself on one of 175 rosewood chairs and enjoy such exotic oriental delicacies as bird's nest soup, abalone and snake. The hotel rents cellular phones for a quick call to check on the folks back home.

Pan Pacific, 999 Canada Place (tel: 662-8111). The sparkling 505-room Pan Pacific, the tower adjacent to the white sails at Canada Place overlooking

Burrard Inlet, is spectacular. Every room has a water view. The white sails housing the Convention Centre have become a city symbol, much the same as the Opera House in Sydney.

Westin Bayshore, 1601 West Georgia Street (tel: 682-3377). Vancouver's only downtown resort hotel, The Bayshore hugs the huddle of yachts moored in Coal Harbour. Most of the 519 units offer breathtaking views of the mountains, harbour and city. The Somerset Maughamesque Garden Lounge and world-famous Trader Vic's restaurant (which serves the best Caesar salad in the city) are wonderful.

Moderately Priced Hotels

The following hotels (priced from about C$60 per double) offer comfortable and clean accommodation. Some have mountain and water views. When making reservations, be sure to enquire about seasonal, seniors' and other discounts.

Barclay Hotel, 1348 Robson Street (tel: 688-8850). This small, European-style hotel (85 rooms) has a licensed lounge and a recently renovated dining room.

Blue Horizon, 1225 Robson Street (tel: 688-1411). Many of the 214 units in this hotel have panoramic views and private balconies, fridges and coffee makers. Hotel amenities include a lap pool, jacuzzi, sauna, exercise equipment, coffee shop and lounge.

Park Royal Hotel, 440 Clyde Avenue, West Vancouver (tel: 926-5511). Located north across the Lion's Gate Bridge, about five miles (8km) from downtown

Horsepower still exists, even outside the modern Pan Pacific

Vancouver, the Park Royal is a romantic mock-Tudor building with only 30 rooms. This oasis of tranquillity on the west bank of the Capilano River is a 10-minute bus ride from city centre. But it is only a five-minute walk to Park Royal Shopping Centre, an indoor complex of 190 stores. Ambleside Beach is a short stroll away. Both the dining room and the pub overlook a beautiful old English garden. Complimentary morning coffee or tea and a newspaper.

Quality Inn, 1335 Howe Street

ACCOMMODATION

(tel: 682-0229). The Quality Inn is a 10-minute walk from downtown and a five-minute mini-ferry ride from Granville Island. Some of the 153 units are apartments. Amenities include an outdoor heated pool, a restaurant and lounge. Wheelchair accessible.

Sands Motor Inn, 1755 Davie Street (tel: 682-1831). This Best Western property has 119 units. The lounge looks out to English Bay. The hotel has some kitchen-units, a restaurant and a sauna and fitness centre. Some rooms are noisy, especially during summer weekends.

Sunset Inn, 1111 Burnaby Street (tel: 684-8763). Close to downtown, the English Bay Beaches and Stanley Park, all 50 condominium suites have fully equipped kitchens. Weekly and monthly rates available mid-June to mid-September.

Sylvia Hotel, 1154 Gilford Street (tel: 681-9321). The Sylvia is an ivy-clad brick heritage building overlooking English Bay at the entrance to Stanley Park. The hotel has some housekeeping suites, a restaurant and lounge overlooking English Bay.

Budget Hotels
Downtown budget hotels (from about C$40 a double) vary a great deal in quality. Generally speaking, those west of downtown are cleaner and more secure.

Buchan Hotel, 1906 Haro Street (tel: 685-5354). Most rooms have private baths and cable TV but no phones. The hotel houses Delilah's, one of Vancouver's best restaurants.

The **Kingston Hotel**, 757 Richards Street (tel: 684-9024), includes a continental breakfast in the room rate. The hotel also features sauna, laundry and optional TV. Off-season, seniors' and student rates available.

The **YMCA**, 955 Burrard Street (tel: 681-0221) and the **YWCA**, 580 Burrard Street (tel: 662-8188)

Delilah's at the Buchan Hotel, just a block from Stanley Park

hotels are both good downtown bargains. Couples are welcome at both hotels. The YWCA has a pool and fitness centre for female guests.

Youth Hostels
The **Vancouver Youth Hostel** at 1515 Discovery Street (tel: 224-3208) is the only hostel within the city. Just a short stroll from beautiful Jericho Beach, the 300-bed hostel is the largest in Canada and offers accommodation to members of the International Youth Hostel Association. Family rooms and kitchens are available. A cafeteria provides inexpensive meals. A new lounge, featuring satellite screen television, is a fine place to socialise with fellow travellers. Other facilities include personal lockers and laundry room.

University Accommodation
Both **Simon Fraser University** (tel: 291-4201), on Burnaby Mountain, 12 miles (20km) east of city centre, and the **University of British Columbia**, at 5961 Student Union Boulevard (tel: 228-2963), 10 miles (16km) southwest of the city centre, offer summer housing from May to August. Both offer single furnished rooms with shared bath. UBC also has a studio, one- and two-bedroom suites with private bathrooms and kitchenettes.

Bed and Breakfast Accommodation
Metropolitan Vancouver is home to a great number of bed and breakfast establishments, many of them born with EXPO 86. Some come and go. Most are found in suburban residential

areas; few are downtown. But it's a good way to meet the locals. Some B&Bs are luxurious, some are spartan. Some have private bath, some have shared bath. Some are farmhouses and some are townhouses. Weekly and monthly rates are often available. A dozen booking agencies belong to the **British Columbia Bed and Breakfast Association**, Box 593, 810 West Broadway, Vancouver V5Z 4E2 (tel: 276-8616). Owner Helen Burich of **Town & Country B&B** inspects homes personally and sells her book of listings from PO Box 46544, Vancouver V6R 4G8 (tel: 731-5942). A favourite is **Billy Wittmann's on the Beach**, at 4550 North West Marine Drive (tel: 224-2177), which offers German-style hospitality in a modern double A-frame home.

Campgrounds
In good weather, the best bargain accommodation in town is the modern **Capilano Mobile Park**, 295 Tomahawk Avenue (tel: 987-4722). After a half-hour hike from downtown, you can pitch your tent here, right on the east bank of the Capilano River. Half a dozen restaurants and several grocery stores and 180 other shops are a five-minute walk away in the Park Royal Shopping Centre. The campground is surprisingly quiet, considering that it nestles in a traffic arm approaching the Lion's Gate Bridge. Features include 24-hour-a-day super-vision, laundromat, the Cedar Room with a 10-person jacuzzi, an outdoor swimming pool, a TV lounge with video games, and some spectacular totems.

NIGHTLIFE AND ENTERTAINMENT

Few people come to Vancouver for the nightlife, except perhaps in winter and spring, when avid skiers slalom the slopes of the North Shore mountains under the stars. But the city has a great variety of indoor nightlife, featuring local, national and international talent in opera, ballet, classical music, rock, jazz, theatre and cinema. The daily newspapers, the *Vancouver Sun* and the *Province*, and the complimentary weeklies, the *West Ender* and the *Georgia Strait*, contain advertising listings and editorial reviews of current entertainment. The compact monthly magazine, *Key to Vancouver*, which is free in most hotels, provides detailed information on musical and theatrical performances, along with listings of cabarets, clubs, jazz spots and good dining and dancing places. The **Arts Hotline** (tel: 684-ARTS) provides information on the performing arts; and the **Coastal Jazz and Blues Society** (tel: 682-0706) offers information on current and forthcoming jazz events. For recorded information on current movies and locations, call **Cineplex Odeon** (tel: 687-1515), **Famous Players** (tel: 681-4255) or the individual independent cinemas.

Tickets

The **Vancouver Travel Infocentre** (tel: 683-2000), at 1055 Dunsmuir Street, sells tickets to

Vancouver's night-time glamour can be found both indoors and out

cultural and sporting events, as does **Ticketmaster** (tel: 280-4444), which has outlets in Eaton's department stores throughout the city. Ticketmaster has special lines for arts events (tel: 280-3311) and spectator sports (tel: 280-4400), in case the main line is busy, as it often is. Cinema tickets are sold at the individual movie theatres.

Classical Concerts, Ballet and Opera

Many musical events are held at the gracious and elegant **Orpheum**. Originally built as a vaudeville hall in 1927, the Orpheum, located on Smithe Street at Granville (tel: 665-3035), is now the official home of the Vancouver Symphony Orchestra. The 2,800-seat **Queen Elizabeth Theatre**, at 630

Hamilton Street, hosts touring musicals, concerts, opera, ballet and other dance artists. The adjacent **Playhouse** holds Sunday morning coffee concerts, with in-house babysitting available at a minimum charge. Other musical events take place at the **Vancouver East Cultural Centre**, at 1895 Venables Street. Free noon-hour concerts are often held on the plaza in **Robson Square** during July and August. The Vancouver Recital Society performs regularly in the Playhouse and the Orpheum. Headphones for people with hearing disabilities are available at the Queen Elizabeth Theatre, the Playhouse and at the Orpheum. All these places are wheelchair accessible.

Theatre

The **Arts Club Theatre** (tel: 687-1644) is the most active theatre in town, with two venues (including a revue theatre) on Granville Island. Also popular are the **Waterfront Theatre** on Granville Island (tel: 685-6217) and the **Vancouver East Cultural Centre**, at 1895 East Venables Street (tel: 254-9578). Performances at these locales vary from classical Shakespeare to popular drama and contemporary works by local playwrights. At the small **Back Alley Theatre**, at 751 Thurlow Street (tel: 688-7013), the Theatre Sports League involves the audience in improvisational comedy, Tuesday to Saturday at 20.00 hrs. **Punchlines**, at 15 Water Street (tel: 684-3015), offers clean stand-up comedy Monday to Saturday at 21.00 hrs; the unlicensed Comedy Cellar downstairs entertains youths who have not yet reached the BC drinking age of 19. **Theatre Under The Stars** (tel: 687-0174) has been putting on popular plays and musicals for half a century at the Malkin Bowl bandstand in Stanley Park from June to August, weather permitting; it's especially fun with a picnic thermos under a full moon.

Jazz

Some of the city's best jazz artists prefer the intimate **Alma Street Café**, at 2505 Alma Street (tel: 222-2244), where the music plays from 20.00 hrs Wednesday to Saturday; the food and service are excellent (reservations advised). At **Carnegie's Bar and Grill**, at 1619 West Broadway (tel: 733-4141), mainstream jazz pianist Bob Murghy and various guests entertain. The relatively new **Glass Slipper**, at 185 East Eleventh Street (tel: 872-0233), is a cooperative rehearsal and performance hall for local and imported talent; public performances are limited and quality varies. **Chardonnay's**, at 808 West Hastings Street (tel: 684-1511), has jazz Thursday to Saturday 21.00–01.00 hrs. The **Rattlesnake Grill**, at 2340 West Fourth Avenue (tel: 733-2911), offers jazz and blues every night from 19.00 hrs, along with fine dining on such delicacies as smoked rattlesnake in a comfortable southwestern adobe setting; reservations recommended. The **Troller**, at 6422 Bay Street in Horseshoe Bay (tel: 921-7616), is a popular Saturday afternoon spot for live jazz. The annual **Du Maurier**

International Jazz Festival is held in June, usually at the Vancouver East Cultural Centre at 1895 Venables Street. For more information, call the **Jazz Hotline** (tel: 682-0706).

Rock and Contemporary Music

Big Canadian and international music groups entertain at **BC Place Stadium**, which seats 60,000 people, and the **Pacific Coliseum**, on the PNE grounds. Smaller places to hear name bands and local talent include the **Commodore Ballroom**, at 870 Granville Street (tel: 681-7838), and **86 Street**, at 750 Pacific Boulevard (tel: 683-8687).

Discos and Nightclubs

Amnesia, at 99 Powell Street (tel: 682-2211), is a multi-level Gatsby-style club with several bars and video screens. You can dance to the Top 40 as well as classics from years past. **Club Soda**, at 1055 Homer Street (tel: 681-8202), features theatre seating, videos and live music, with a good dance floor. **Richards on Richards** (tel: 687-6794) offers live entertainment, recorded music, videos and both snack and dinner menus. **The Town Pump**, at 66 Water Street (tel: 683-6695), is a favourite with locals, who like the local and imported bands and the extensive selection of beer and videos; a full dinner menu is available.

Cinemas

Vancouver has dozens of movie theatres showing the latest feature films. Most are located downtown on the Granville Street Mall, and there are 10 little cinemas in the Royal Centre Mall. The **Pacific Cinematique**, at

A city sight alight at night: the glittering Science World

1131 Howe Street (tel: 688-8202), is a non-profit educational society devoted to the enjoyment and study of film; the main emphasis is on non-commercial film, including such classics as *Alphaville* and *La Notte de San Lorenzo*. **The Ridge**, at 3131 Arbutus Street (tel: 738-6311), also features the classical and offbeat, serves delicious carrot cake and cappuccino, and has a crying room for the kiddies. The annual **Vancouver International Film Festival** takes place early October. In-room hotel television sets offer entertainment from more than a dozen channels, as well as a selection of pay-TV movies. If you have a VCR, you can rent thousands of videos (mostly VHS) from shops scattered throughout the city. Check the Yellow Pages of the Vancouver phone book.

Dinner Plus
La Quena Coffee House, at 1111 Commercial Drive (tel: 251-6626), serves reasonably priced dinners from 17.00–22.00 hrs daily except Monday; entertainment varies from videos to live performances by Guatemalan singers. The ultra-modern **Soft Rock Café**, at 1925 West Fourth Avenue (tel: 736-8480), serves a set menu followed by entertainment; the meal is rarely the highlight of the evening. Try to catch talented local chanteuse Joelle Rabu. **The Blarney Stone**, at 216 Carrall Street (tel: 687-4322), is a lively Gastown restaurant with Irish and contemporary entertainment; the music starts at 21.00 hrs nightly. At **Mulvaney's**, on Granville Island (tel: 685-6571), the tasty Cajun cuisine is complemented at 21.00–01.00 hrs nightly by disc jockey music for dancing. **The Roof**, just under the copper roof of the Vancouver Hotel (tel: 684-3131), serves good food to the tunes of local musicians playing swing, big band, light jazz and old favourites, 20.30–24.00 hrs Tuesday to Saturday.

Casinos
Gambling is highly regulated in Canada, but a few operations such as the **Great Canadian Casino**, in the Holiday Inn at 711 West Broadway (tel: 291-WINS), have learned to live with the laws. Dice are not permitted, so games are limited to roulette and blackjack. Casinos are open from 18.00–02.00 hrs; non-alcoholic beverages and snacks are available. Fifty per cent of the proceeds go to local charities.

WEATHER

WEATHER AND WHEN TO GO

Vancouver enjoys a moderate climate, thanks in part to warm Pacific currents. There are few extremes in temperature. The highest recorded temperature is 91°F (33°C) and the lowest is 0°F (−18°C). The only extreme is the rain, and winter months, especially November, December and January, can be very wet and grey. But this is the rainforest. While only 40 inches (100cm) of rain fall on the airport each year, the North Shore suburbs, cradled by the coastal mountains,receive as much as 100 inches (250cm) a year. The summer months of June, July and August are usually the driest and sunniest. Monthly hours of sunshine average 305 (63 per cent of the total possible) in July and 44 hours in December. For a recorded weather report day or night, call **Environment Canada** (tel: 666-1087), which also predicts the possibility of rain or snow falling.

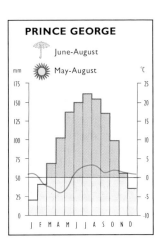

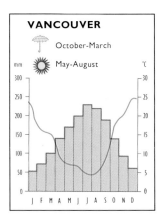

What to Bring

Vancouverites, who wear both formal and informal dress, depending on the occasion, may be a little more mellow than their eastern counterparts. Almost anything goes, any time. Some women wear fox fur jackets and sandals to the office, while others wear anoraks and running shoes. Shorts for both sexes are acceptable leisure wear in summer, but a sweater is often welcome after the sun settles over the Pacific. An umbrella, raincoat and waterproof footwear can be handy any time of the year, but more so in winter. Layered clothes are most practical, especially for venturing up the North Shore mountains. Don't worry if you haven't brought what you need, for practically everything is sold here.

When to Go

Any time is a good time to visit. But if steel skies and wet

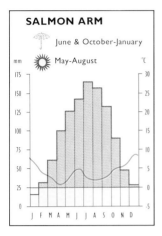

SALMON ARM

June & October-January

May-August

weather bother you, you'd better gamble on the drier and sunnier summer.

The Dr Sun Yat-Sen Classical Chinese Garden, the Museum of Anthropology and a walk in the rainforest seem equally beautiful in rainy weather, and for such sites as the Science Centre, the weather simply doesn't matter at all. Winter rains at sea level have their advantages; they often mean snow on the mountains, so skiers like winter best. Mountain lifts frequently soar right above the clouds to sunshine. The longer and sunnier spring days, when the mountains still wear their white caps, let skiers and sunbathers in swimsuits savour both the sun and snow. While summer sees the city crowded with visitors, sun seekers can relax on the sunny beaches and enjoy the longer evenings when the sun doesn't set until after the Nine O'Clock Gun in Stanley Park booms out the time.

HOW TO BE A LOCAL

Although the official languages of Canada are English and French, there are only about 50,000 French-speaking Vancouverites. English is the main language of the city. Cantonese is common, as about 100,000 Chinese people live in Vancouver. Vancouverites come from more than 60 cultural groups and speak as many languages. Almost half the children in city schools are studying English as a second language. Vancouverites are Caucasian and Oriental, native Indian and East Indian, and some are from the West Indies and Africa. Some are as urbane as sophisticated New Yorkers, while others are simply farmers and fisherfolk. So no matter where you're from, hide your camera and you'll look like a local.

Sometimes described as conservative Californians, Vancouverites are more reserved than Americans, even though the Washington State border lies only 30 miles (50km) south. Canadians wear slightly less flashy clothes, are a little less chatty, and rarely laugh out loud at movies the way Americans do. To speak Canadian English, you need only to add 'eh' to the end of a sentence, as in 'It's a nice day, eh?' This may be a remnant of the French Canadian *n'est-ce pas* influence.

Service in Vancouver hotels, shops and restaurants does not match the superior service of the Orient, perhaps because Canadians are reluctant to complain. If you step on someone's foot, and he or she

HOW TO BE A LOCAL

apologises, you can be sure you've bumped into a genuine Canadian. Vancouver is a young city, only a hundred years old, and is just beginning to realise that training is required for the front-line troops in the hospitality industry. Consequently, clerks and waiters sometimes have little idea of what is going on. If you encounter sloppy service and do not complain, people will assume you are Canadian. Sometimes it's not smart to be too much like a local.

Canadian couples are used to sleeping in double beds, so the hotel clerk may look askance when a couple requests twin beds. While business people on expense accounts often order three-course meals, most locals make do with less.

Vancouverites usually eat salads before the main course; and west coast salads with lots of flower blossoms and wild grasses are currently in vogue. Although blind tastings indicate that British Columbia produces some excellent wines, Vancouverites tend to order wines imported from the western American states, Europe, Australia, New Zealand, Chile, and even Ontario.

Vancouverites usually queue at bus stops and taxi stands. Pedestrians tend to cross at crosswalks, as they have the right of way at intersections. Smoking on the street, once considered bad form, is now common, as most office buildings do not permit smoking, even in lounge areas. While Vancouverites pretend to be puritan at times, the doorman at almost every downtown hotel will accept a five-dollar tip and keep your car near by for you at no additional charge.

Vancouverites rarely honk their car horns, even when the traffic is reminiscent of downtown Istanbul at rush hour: it is a ticketable offence. The 'Tiddley Cove Two-Step' should be preserved on video as a remnant of a dying era. The Two-Step describes the approach to the Lion's Gate Bridge from North and West Vancouver. During rush hour and at other times during the winter when there are few visitors about, cars politely take turns alternating into a single stream of traffic. But during the crowded summer season, everyone tries to merge before each other and the system collapses.

Vancouverites tell other Canadians that it rains all the time here, so that they won't feel so bad about having to suffer long snowy winters, only to be bitten by the mammoth mosquitoes of springtime. On the quiet, residents of Vancouver admit that their city is the most beautiful one in the world, but many rarely venture out into the great outdoors during the dark and rainy days of winter. Others jog compulsively right through thunderstorms without losing pace. In the rain, it's a little easier to distinguish the locals: they are usually the ones without umbrellas, raincoats and waterproof footwear. Vancouver men, especially, shun umbrellas. Vancouverites buy BMWs and then try to save a buck or two by taking advantage of advertised specials, so queues form early at such promotions as Safeway's

How to be a local: join the queues of hungry Vancouverites at the nearest popcorn stall

once-a-month $1.49 day. Locals love garage sales and flea markets. Weekend newspapers list garage sales throughout the city. Or drive through a residential neighbourhood on Saturday or Sunday, where garage sale signs lead to the locations. By rummaging through old hotel ashtrays, musty clothes and a few tattered lamps that haven't seen light in decades, cultivated consumers occasionally find genuine bargains, and enjoy the cultural experience. The **Vancouver Flea Market**, at 703 Terminal Avenue (tel: 685-0666), is open Saturday and Sunday, 09.00–16.00 hrs. Where all kinds of trucks and trailers with little doors marked 'make-up' and 'wardrobe' block a street, you can be sure someone is shooting a movie.

Linger with the locals on the edge of the set and watch the action or promise of action. The BC film industry is thriving. Such television favourites as *MacGyver* are frequently filmed downtown.

The wet wilderness in springtime brings pussywillows to decorate your hotel room. During the summer, put a plastic bucket in your rental car and head south to Richmond (30 minutes) or east to the Fraser Valley (30 minutes) to pick berries, which make great snacks for a day or two. Strawberries are generally ripe mid-June to mid-July, raspberries during July and blueberries mid-July to mid-September. Prices are about half retail prices. Lush juicy blackberries, free for the picking, line many roadsides in August. In October, pick up a pumpkin for a dollar or two and carve it into a haunting face for

Hallowe'en. Locals love to lounge around the public libraries scattered throughout the city. The main library, at the corner of Burrard and Robson Streets downtown, frequently features seasonal celebrations and readings by local authors. Non-residents may purchase a temporary library card, half the cost of which is refundable. And the **National Film Board**, at 1045 Howe Street (tel: 666-0716), houses a range of 800 VHS video tapes, varying from short animations to lengthy documentaries on social issues. Another good way to look like a local is by participating in special events. Almost every weekend sees a fund-raising walk or run of some sort. If this pastime is too tepid, join the 2,000 Vancouverites who splash into English Bay on New Year's Day for the annual Polar Bear Swim. The water temperature is a cool 40°F (4°C). If the water's too wet, try cross-country skiing in Cypress Bowl (30 minutes northwest), where both rentals and instruction are available. Or join the crowds in Chinatown for the colourful Chinese New Year's parade in February. In the springtime, join hundreds of local dogwalkers in a pooch parade in Stanley Park. The annual **Teddy Bear Parade and Picnic** (tel: 432-6350) is a family affair held every August at Deas Island Regional Park in Delta. To finish off the year, join the locals at First Night, a New Year's Eve celebration downtown, where hordes of Vancouverites roam the streets enjoying various outdoor and indoor entertainment.

PERSONAL PRIORITIES

Like most big cities, Vancouver supplies everything you are likely to need, and you will not find it necessary to pack a vast amount of nappies, tampons, or other personal items before leaving home. There are ample shopping facilities in Vancouver; pharmacies are plentiful, though many are tucked away at the back of big drugstores, and you may need to hunt a bit for them! The wide range of bars

*A Granville Island cyclist shows a
novel way of avoiding traffic jams*

and night clubs available means
that most people should find
somewhere to suit their tastes.
If you plan to travel in the wide
open spaces, you may find it best
to stock up on required items
before you set out.
For addresses and telephone
numbers of pharmacies which
open seven days a week, see
Pharmacist in the **Directory**,
page 115.

CHILDREN

Vancouver and environs offer a
variety of attractions to entertain
and educate the young—and the
young at heart. Some activities
listed here are described in
more detail in other sections of
this book. Check the Friday
'Family Fun' column in the
Vancouver Sun or Daniel Wood's
book, *Kids! Kids! Kids! in
Vancouver*, for further
suggestions. If you're driving, all
you need is a map, a kindly
concierge to give directions and
a pocketful of quarters for
parking. If you're taking the
family by bus, call **BC Transit**
(tel: 261-5100) for information.
Camp Hyatt at the Hyatt
Regency Hotel in downtown
Vancouver (tel: 800-233-1234 toll-
free world-wide) provides
reduced rates for families, and
children's menus in restaurants
and room service. The Camp
Hyatt Passport, available for
children aged three to 15,
provides puppet shows, movies,
arts and crafts, sing-alongs and a
mid-evening snack, from
18.00–22.00 hrs Friday and
Saturday. The hotel concierge
keeps games for children to
borrow. The Delta Place Hotel
(tel: 687-1122) also has a
supervised children's activity
centre. And most hotels have
reliable babysitters.

Downtown
CN IMAX Theatre, at Canada
Place (tel: 682-4629), is a 500-seat
cinema, with a five-storey-high
wrap-around screen and superb
sound. Five diverse and
delightful short films on scenics,
sports adventures and space
travel are shown daily.

CHILDREN

The Imagination Market, at 528 Powell Street (tel: 253-1033), recycles such leftovers as mylar, Belgian lace, bits of rubber and wood, film cannisters and computer ribbon spools, so that children can spend happy hours creating everything from hats to helicopters. Imaginative parents have fun, too. Drop-in workshops on Saturday and Sunday 12.00–16.00 hrs. A non-profit retail store sells recycled materials 11.00–17.00 hrs Thursday to Sunday.

Science World, at 1445 Quebec Street (tel: 687-7832), provides enough hands-on education and entertainment for a whole day, and has a cafeteria on site for lunch. Children and adults can blow big square bubbles, feel a frozen flower, and type their names into a computer and then hear them set to music. The centre also houses an OMNIMAX cinema, where a large domed screen, surrounded by a 28,000-watt 28-speaker sound system, presents six shows daily.

Stanley Park. In addition to the polar bears and playful otters, children love the Petting Zoo (tel: 681-1141) and the Miniature Railway (open 11.00-16.00 hrs daily), which chugs along through a mini-wilderness of kangaroos, peacocks, wolves and bighorn sheep. At the **Aquarium** (tel: 685-3364), children enjoy the tidal pools, where they can pat sea cucumbers, anemones, star fishes and chitons, and they love sitting close to the killer whale shows, where the mammoth mammals feed and splash water on anyone close by.

For more water fun, there are water parks on the seawall near

Children can get close to nature in the Stanley Park Petting Zoo

Lumberman's Arch and near the fire engine playground near Pacific Avenue. And in summer there is lifeguarded swimming at the pool at Second Beach. Bicycles, which can also burn away extra energy, are rented at the Georgia Street entrance to the park, on the scenic seawall. **Vancouver East Cultural Centre**, at 1895 Venables Street (tel: 254-9578), features such favourite films as *The Black Stallion* and *Winnie The Pooh*, especially for children, at 13.00 hrs on Saturdays. Pay what you can.

Granville Island

First stop in this area, accessible via the little False Creek ferries from the south end of downtown, should be the **Information Centre**, at 1592 Johnston Street (tel: 666-5784), open 09.00–18.00 hrs daily. Keeping in mind that children are usually more contented when their mouths are full, head to the **Public Market** (open 09.00–18.00 hrs daily; closed Monday in winter) to feast on everything from fresh mangoes to wholesome Vietnamese salad rolls and pasty doughnuts. The fudge-maker is fun to watch, and in good weather jugglers and colourful clowns entertain on the waterfront. While walking through the streets of Granville Island, you can peer through windows and watch craftsmen at work. The **Kids Only Market**, at 1496 Cartwright Street (tel: 689-8447), houses two dozen shops, varying from 'Knotty Toys' to 'The Everything Wet Store' (open daily 10.00–18.00 hrs June to August; closed Monday the rest of the year) and a Playcare

Centre for youngsters aged three to five.

At the supervised summertime **Water Park**, children douse each other with big fire hoses hitched to revolving hydrants; parents can watch while sipping a cappuccino at nearby **Isadora's**, a reasonably priced restaurant with a children's play area inside.

The **Arts Umbrella**, at 1286 Cartwright Street (tel: 681-5268), runs two-week day camps in July for children up to age 18 (09.00–16.00 hrs with shorter days for pre-schoolers), developing such skills as painting, drawing, wood-carving and acting; reservations advised. Families can share outdoor fun with kayaks rented from **Ecomarine**, at 1668 Duranleau Street (tel: 689-7575), and paddle around the Granville Island area.

University of British Columbia

At the **Museum of Anthropology** (tel: 228-5087), children can beat the hanging drums and pull out dozens of drawers to 'ooh' and 'aah' at all the West Coast Indian toys, jewellery and clothing. Children enjoy Bill Reid's classic carving of *The Raven and the First Man*, especially if you read the legend to them.

It's fun to feed the fish at **Nitobe Gardens** and watch a *tai chi* demonstration at the nearby **Asian Centre**. And in summer, watch cows being milked at the **UBC Dairy Barns** (tel: 228-4593). Resident astronomers at **The Observatory** (tel: 228-2267) provide an exciting evening looking at planets and the stars, and let the children jump on the floor to create an 'earthquake' on

the continuously running seismic recorder.

Pacific Spirit Park (tel: 432-6350), which surrounds UBC, offers weekend programmes with park interpreters on such subjects as slugs and edible wild plants.
Teas & Tarts outings include nature walks along forested trails, with maybe mint tea and blackberry tarts served in a clearing at the end of the tour. From UBC, a ribbon of beaches laces the south shore of English Bay and has many great places for barbecues and delicatessen picnics. The **Jericho Sailing Centre**, at 1300 Discovery Street (tel: 224-4177), has a good summer programme for

Muster up your courage for a stroll on Capilano suspension bridge

teaching children to sail. They sail almost bathtub-sized craft, while an instructor whizzes around in a zodiac keeping everyone up to speed. On the nearby pier, kids enjoy watching crab fishermen inspect the little critters, to ascertain whether they're big enough to keep.

East Vancouver and Burnaby
The rides at **Playland**, on the PNE (Pacific National Exhibition) grounds (tel: 255-5161), are open in summer. Never mind that the horses on the antique carousels need painting and are falling apart. Never mind that Mum has

to close her eyes in terror at the sight of workmen repairing the log chute while she and her family are on it. Kids love the rollercoasters, candyfloss and taffy apples. For a calmer day, children can watch the log-rolling contests, chickens hatching, cows calving and free rock concerts at the PNE, which takes place during the last two weeks of August.

Chuck E Cheese, at 9898 Government Avenue in Burnaby (tel: 421-8408), is a mini-Disneyland with a ballroom with a deep pool of 20,000 balls, a tinker tower of slides and ladders for little ones, a video parlour, three mechanical orchestras and inexpensive food; open 10.30–21.00 hrs daily.

Toys Plus More, at 6508 East Hastings Street in Burnaby (tel: 298-6970), houses thousands of toys. You use a black garbage bag to fill with your purchases. Open 09.30–17.30 Monday to Saturday, with hours extended to 21.00 on Thursdays and Fridays.

North Shore

Children can sway on old suspension bridges at both **Capilano** and **Lynn Canyons**, ride the big gondola up **Grouse Mountain**, join a fishing charter at **Sewell's Marina** in Horseshoe Bay, and in summer ride the vintage **Royal Hudson** steam train north to Squamish.

If all this is too much for you, or your young ones, call the **YMCA** (tel: 251-1116) and arrange for your children (age 6–16) to savour the simple life of a summer wilderness camp, where counsellors care for them (from about C\$300 a week).

TIGHT BUDGET

Budget travellers are sure to enjoy Vancouver. Spectacular water and mountain views in almost every direction are free for the looking. Vancouver sits on the edge of the great continent of capitalism, so promotions of one kind or another abound. There are discounts for children, for students, for families, for seniors and for your uncle who served in the French Foreign Legion. Specials are advertised in such publications as the *Vancouver Province*, the *Vancouver Sun*, the *Westender* (free), the *Georgia Strait* (free) and the *Key to Vancouver* (free; available in most hotels).

Food

Breakfast is the best bargain of the day. Coffee shop windows downtown advertise bacon, eggs, toast and coffee (usually no charge for refills) for a few dollars; stick to the advertised specials, though, because substitutions often cost extra. The best breakfast and lunch value in town may be the Cantonese *dim sum*. Chinatown restaurants start serving *dim sum* as early as 07.00 hrs and continue until 14.00 hrs. Waitresses wheel around carts laden with dozens of varieties of such tasty morsels as steamed dumplings filled with prawns, spring rolls and lemon tarts. Point to whatever you want. It's a challenge to eat 10 dollars' worth of *dim sum*. The usual charge is half that. Tea is complimentary and, to order more, just leave the lid on the teapot up.

The tiny **Shogun Sapporo**

TIGHT BUDGET

Ramen, 518 Hornby Street, serves inexpensive yet substantial and savoury portions of Japanese garlicky *gyoza*, steaming *ramen* and *teriyaki*. The legendary no frills **Only Café**, 20 East Hastings Street, sells mounds of fish and chips for low prices, although customer queues sometimes stretch out into the street. The **Singapore Restaurant**, 546 West Broadway, serves excellent and inexpensive *nasi goreng, mee goreng* and *saté* lunches. For a romantic candlelight and wine dinner (weeknights only) that doesn't break the bank, try **JJ's**, 250 West Pender Street (tel: 669-9373; reservations recommended) a part of the Vancouver Vocational Institute, where apprentice chefs prepare such *haute cuisine* as rack of New Zealand lamb. Service may be slow, but you're on holiday. **Umbertino's**, an Italian fast-food chain, serves delicious pastas, garlic bread and Caesar salads; eat-in or take-out daily specials are very reasonably priced. Such standard standbys as **McDonalds**, **Wendy's** and **Burger King** found all over the city spare the wallet and spoil the child.

Skip the camembert and vintage cabernet and a picnic in the park can be a bargain. Bring an umbrella for winter weather. Local markets offer everything from bagels with lox and cream cheese to Vietnamese salad rolls with peanut sauce. All taste great eaten on a bench at the market or on a grassy knoll in a nearby park. The restaurant sections of most shopping malls also feature fast-foods. Chinatown bakeries sell delicious curried beef and barbecued pork buns at bargain prices. If you're stocking up for a camping trip to the interior it's worth a trip to $1.49 day at Safeway supermarkets.

Sightseeing

Sightseers who have done their homework can spend weeks here with minimal cost. **China-town** provides a great glimpse of the exotic East. East Pender and Keefer Streets (between Carrall and Gore) are chock-a-block with busy vegetable stalls, meat markets, rattan shops, oriental pharmacies, restaurants and bakeries. Stop for a complimentary cup of jasmine or hibiscus tea at the **Ten Ren Tea and Ginseng Company** (Main at Keefer) or an inexpensive but delicious butterhorn at the **BC Royal Cafe**, 119 East Pender. Browse through colourful food markets on Granville Island, Lonsdale Quay, Westminster Quay and Robson Street. Stroll through the cobblestone streets of old **Gastown**, originally built with gold rush money and restored in the late 1960s, and see and hear the world's largest steam clock chime every quarter hour.

There is no admission charge for the following sights: the **Grocery Hall of Fame**, at 9500 Van Horne Way in Richmond (tel: 278-0665), houses an eclectic collection of old grocery items; open Monday to Friday, 09.00–17.00 hrs; Saturdays 09.00–12.00 hrs. The **BC Sugar Museum**, one block west of Clark Drive at Powell (tel: 253-1131), chronicles the history of Vancouver and the sugar industry; open Monday to Friday, 09.00–15.30 hrs. The

Seeing Gastown's clock letting off steam is a free treat

BC Sports Hall of Fame, on the PNE grounds at Renfrew & Hastings (tel: 253-2311, local 233), shelters 115 showcases of photos, medals and other mementos honouring victories of local athletes; open Monday to Friday, 09.00–16.30 hrs. The **Capilano Salmon Hatchery**, off Capilano Road in North Vancouver (tel: 987-1411), displays coho, steelhead and chinook in various stages of growth and development. From July to November, you can usually watch returning salmon leaping ladders into the hatchery; open daily 08.00–20.00 hrs in summer and until dusk in winter. At the **Lynn Canyon Ecology Centre**, in North Vancouver (tel: 987-5922), you can skip across an old-fashioned suspension bridge spanning a rushing river in the rainforest; open daily 10.00–17.00 hrs, closed weekends in December and January.

Canada Place (tel: 688-TOUR), with the landmark white sails at the north end of Burrard Street, which houses the Trade & Convention Centre, cruise ship docks, various restaurants and the Pan Pacific hotel, offers self-guided tours and occasional guided group tours; open daily 09.00–21.00 hrs May to October and 09.00–17.00 winter. The **Port of Vancouver Viewing Area**, at Vanterm, at the north end of Clark Drive (tel: 666-6129), provides a peek at operations in Canada's largest port; open Tuesday to Friday 09.00–12.00 hrs and 13.00–16.00 hrs for self-directed tours; one-hour guided tours available from June to August at 13.00, 14.00 and 15.00 hrs. Even the parking is free.

The **Vancouver Art Gallery** waives the admission fee on Thursday evenings, 17.00–21.00 hrs, and the **Museum of Anthropology** does the same on Tuesdays all day.

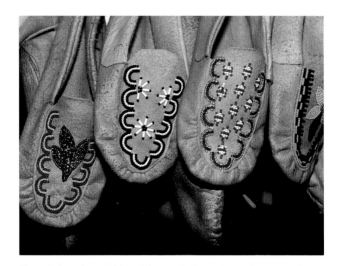

There is free skywatching at the **Gordon Southam Observatory**, 1100 Chestnut Street (tel: 738-2855), on clear Fridays, Saturdays and Sundays; reservations recommended. Admission is by donation to the following attractions: **Irving House**, 302 Royal Avenue, New Westminster (tel: 521-7656), is a heritage home dating from 1864 with furnishings from that era; open May to mid-September 11.00-17.00 hrs and winter weekends 13.00-17.00 hrs. The *Samson V*, built in 1937, was the last sternwheeler to ply the Fraser River and harbours a history of the Fraser Valley during the last century of settlement; open weekends and holidays 12.00–16.00 hrs, more frequently in summer. The tiny **Beatles Museum**, tucked into the back of the Collectors RPM record store at 456 Seymour Street (tel: 685-8841), houses rare memorabilia from the 1960s.

Indian crafts are always a good souvenir idea, and these moccasins are practical, too

Shopping
Browsing has become an acceptable pastime. Both residents and visitors wander through city malls and shops, frequently entertaining themselves by just looking. Sales are advertised in nearly every shop window: closing sales, year-end sales, birthday sales, back-to-school sales ... you name it and somebody has already thought of it. Sales at department stores are the safest bet for bargain-hunters, for if merchandise is defective or you decide you can live without it after all, these stores will refund your money. In Vancouver's smaller shops, they may agree to an exchange, but more often than not you are likely to find that 'all sales are final'.
Department stores advertise

genuine bargains in the weekend newspapers. Occasionally, real bargains turn up at such out-of-the-way shops as **Armadillo**, 3385 Cambie, and the **Scrupulous Boutique**, 3564 Arbutus, which sell designer fashion from Paris and Milan for up to 80 per cent off. Suburban garage sales, usually held on weekend mornings, lend insight into the local way of life and sometimes offer great deals. The **Vancouver Flea Market**, at 703 Terminal Avenue (tel: 685-0666), is open on Saturdays, Sundays and holidays 09.00–16.00 hrs and is a great place to browse and pick up both usual and unusual souvenirs. At the **Robert Held Gallery**, at 2130 Pine Street, Canada's largest glass-blowing studio, big burly men create delicate bud vases and atomizers while you watch. **Jade World**, at 1696 West First Avenue, offers complimentary tours of its studio, where skilled artisans are at work; a wide selection of jade, from tiny trinkets to quality sculptures are for sale; British Columbia has the world's largest known jade deposits. **Manhattan Books**, at 1089 Robson (tel: 681-9074), sell remaindered books, usually at 50 per cent off.

Entertainment

Cineplex Odeon cinemas are half-price throughout the city on Tuesday evenings; some cinemas offer reduced matinée prices. Various theatres offer 50 per cent off or two-for-one price matinées, previews and dress rehearsals. At the annual Fringe Festival in September, which comprises everything from Shakespeare to alternative theatre, prices are about half those charged for regular professional productions. Check local newspapers for dates and times. **Presentation House**, in North Vancouver, frequently offers excellent productions at about half the price of downtown theatres. Video rental shops scattered throughout the city rent both Beta and VHS tapes of recent movies for a few dollars. However, you may not need outside entertainment as any television, with a converter, brings in about 30 channels. Summer sees free dancing at **Robson Square**: big band dancing on Fridays and square dancing on Tuesdays from 20.00–23.00 hrs; and also near **Second Beach** in Stanley Park. There are frequently noon-hour concerts throughout the city, especially in summer. At the Sunday Coffee Concerts at **Queen Elizabeth Playhouse**, all year round, there is a small admission charge and complimentary coffee. The **University of British Columbia** music department (tel: 228-3113) gives complimentary concerts from September to March. One of the best musical bargains around is **CBC FM Radio**, at 105.7 on the dial. The musical selections are almost always excellent, particularly during Jurgen Gothe's Disc Drive, from 15.00–18.00 hrs on weekdays. **La Quena Coffee Shop**, 1111 Commercial Drive (tel: 251-6626), offers Canadian and Latin American folk music on Friday and Saturday evenings; token admission charge. Local libraries, school boards, colleges and universities frequently offer free lectures on a variety of topics; it's advisable to check local newspapers for dates and places.

Take a cheap but enjoyable trip on a Granville Island Ferry

Gardens, Parks and Beaches

Vancouver is home to more than 150 parks and 10 beaches, and they are all free. Many parks have public tennis courts with no charge. Contact the **Vancouver Parks Board** (tel: 681-1141) for more information. The six-mile (9km)-long Stanley Park Seawall is a wonderful walkway; cycling is permitted on the seawall in a counter-clockwise direction only; bicycles can be rented at **Stanley Park Rentals** (tel: 681-5581), near the Georgia Street park entrance.

Transport

Several car rental companies offer various discounts and promotions throughout the year. Budget Rent-a-Car coupons are good for many attractions, hotels and restaurants. **Common Sense Car Rentals**, 225 Kingsway (tel: 877-0999), rents five-year-old vehicles for a reasonable daily charge, plus a 'per-kilometre' supplement, which may be the best deal in town.

Such companies as **Northstar Boat Rentals**, in the Barbary Coast Yacht Basin near Canada Place (tel: 669-5642), rent easy-to-operate four-passenger motor boats at prices which are quite a bargain, considering the exhilaration of exploring the harbour and other waterways; no special licences required. Kayaks, windsurfers and sailing boats, for rent on Granville Island, need no fuel. **Granville Island Ferries** (tel: 684-7781) shuttles passengers between the Aquatic Centre on Beach Avenue and the Arts Club Theatre on Granville Island; this five-minute aquatic adventure is very inexpensive.. The rainbow-roofed **AquaBus** (tel: 874-9930) provides a service between the False Creek Yacht Club and the Arts Club Theatre.

Vancouver's public transit system (tel: 261-5100), one of the world's most scenic, includes buses, the elevated and computerised Skytrain and the SeaBus, a twin-hulled catamaran. Three-day Explorer Passes and one-day passes sell at reduced rates and are valid on the entire system. The Horseshoe Bay bus (board downtown on Georgia Street) provides a breathtaking half-hour ride along Marine Drive in West Vancouver to Horseshoe Bay, where ferries depart for the journey to Vancouver Island.

Accommodation

See **Accommodation**, Budget Hotels, page 82.

SPECIAL EVENTS

Vancouver seems to have
festivals going on all the time,
especially since EXPO 86 set the
stage for successful celebrations.
Although several popular events
take place in summer, when
many tourists are in town, off-
season celebrations are often
more fun because locals then
have more time to laugh.

January

The **Polar Bear Swim** on New
Year's Day is a chilling way to
begin the year. But at least one
Chinese Canadian believes that

*Vancouver knows how to have an
explosive celebration*

participation brings good luck.
While more than 2,000
Vancouverites and visitors
plunge into the frigid waters of
English Bay, an even greater
number of spectators enjoys the
show.

February

Vancouver's 100,000 Chinese
residents throw a great party to
celebrate the **Chinese New
Year**. The highlight is the
Dragon Parade through the
streets of Chinatown, where all

SPECIAL EVENTS

the noise, colour, food and fireworks add to the drama of the dancing dragons eating lucky money wrapped in lettuce leaves by local merchants.

May
The **Vancouver Children's Festival**, held in candy-striped tents in Vanier Park, presents acrobats from China, theatre groups from Spain, and mime, puppetry, music and dance performances by entertainers from around the world.

June
At the 10-day-long **Du Maurier Jazz Festival**, jazz satirists, swing saxophonists and avant-garde guitarists perform funk and blues at several large shopping malls, the Plaza of Nations and such more intimate spots as the Alma Street Café, the Landmark Jazz Bar, Isadora's, the Yale, the Vancouver East Cultural Centre and the Classical Joint.
The Plaza of Nations and Pacific Place are the sites of the **Canadian International Dragon Boat Festival**, where a frenzy of food, fireworks, street theatre and rock and drum bands is highlighted by a colourful parade of 45-foot (13.5m)-long craft with oarsmen paddling along False Creek.

July
The **Vancouver Sea Festival**, a week of nautical celebrations, includes a sailing regatta and an international food fair on Sunset Beach, and a raft of entertainers ranging from Polynesian dancers and *kung fu* athletes to *a capella* singers and concert bands. The grand finale is the Nanaimo to English Bay **Bathtub Race**, a

bizarre display of daring bravado and technical skill.

August
The three-day **Abbotsford International Air Show** takes place at the Abbotsford airport (an hour's drive east from Vancouver). Highlights include antique and experimental aircraft, skydivers, wing walkers, comedy aerobatics and impressive formation flying by the Canadian Forces Snowbirds and the United States Air Force Thunderbirds.
The **Pacific National Exhibition** takes place at Exhibition Park in East Vancouver during the last two weeks before the school year begins. Events include the Superdog Show, log-rolling contests, high diving and the Miss PNE Pageant. Strolling jugglers, minstrels, mimes and clowns entertain, along with contemporary country, rock, jazz, and other musicians who perform on stage. Playland houses 45 rides for children, complete with candyfloss, ice-cone 'slurpies' and foot-long hot dogs. Creative children particularly love the hands-on play centre, Kids' World.

September
In the **Vancouver Fringe Festival** actors, dancers and musicians produce some 100 shows during the week-long celebrations.

October
Known as Hollywood North for the movies and television shows produced here, Vancouver is a logical site for an **International Film Festival**, with more than 100 films from 40 countries.
The **Vancouver Writers Festival**

Choosing your watersport is plain sailing in Vancouver

is a five-day celebration at Granville Island.

Hallowe'en, on 31 October, is a North American festival, when the young and the young at heart dress up in fanciful costumes and carve pumpkins into haunting faces. The tradition of children going from door to door saying 'trick or treat' and expecting bundles of goodies to fall into their bags has given way to private masquerade parties.

December
The pre-Christmas **Carol Ship Parade** is a flotilla of yachts carrying carollers around the harbour.

The **Yuletide Lights of Hope**, a display of Christmas trees in the lobby of Le Meridien Hotel, is very beautiful. New Year's Eve sees 100,000 Vancouverites attending **First Night**, a series of musical and theatrical events downtown. The countdown to Auld Lang Syne always takes place in the plaza in front of the Art Gallery.

SPORT

Consider local architect Arthur Erickson's caveat: 'Vancouver has the worst weather in the world, and the best climate.' In spite of the rain clouds of winter, Vancouver is a paradise for sports enthusiasts: snowy mountains, evergreen golf courses, cycling and hiking trails, sea beaches and breezes for swimmers and sailors, and rivers and inlets teeming with life for eager anglers and divers.

Land Sports
Bowling If the weather is simply too wet for outdoor action, Vancouver's 20 bowling alleys provide shelter spots for 10-pin and five-pin bowling. Most bowling centres have snack bars or restaurants. Check the Yellow Pages of the Vancouver phone book for places and hours.

Cycling The hour's cycle around the paved perimeter pathway of

SPORT

Stanley Park has become a lifetime memory for millions. The paved trail following the SkyTrain route from the Main Street station to New Westminster passes 32 parks and playgrounds for picnics *en route*. Stanley Park Rentals (tel: 681-5581) and a dozen other downtown companies rent bicycles (including tandems). The annual Gastown Grand Prix bicycle race is on 1 July.

Golf British Columbia's 160 golf courses include 17 in Vancouver that are open to the public. Fraserview Golf Course (tel: 327-3717) is one of the most challenging. To play at private courses, bring a letter of introduction from your home club. Several pitch and putt courses are scattered throughout the city. Those in Stanley Park (tel: 681-8847) and Queen Elizabeth Park (tel: 874-8336) are open all year round. At the Ambleside Pitch and Putt (tel: 922-3818; closed November to February), elegant great blue herons sometimes settle on tall trees near by.

Hiking and Walking Stanley Park, Pacific Spirit Park, near UBC and Lighthouse Park in West Vancouver, hide networks of scenic rainforest wilderness trails. Serious hikers may prefer the Baden Powell Trail, which runs from Horseshoe Bay across the North Shore mountains to Deep Cove. For a short two-hour sampler, try the mostly downhill section, from mid-way up Mount Seymour to Deep Cove, which includes spectacular scenery over Indian Arm and Burrard Inlet to Simon Fraser University on Burnaby Mountain.

Skiing Vancouver's three North Shore mountains, all within a half-hour drive of city centre, have well-developed ski areas. On Grouse Mountain (4,100 feet/1,250m) the view from the Peak, Paradise and Cut runs must be one of the most spectacular sights in the world; skiers look beyond the snow at their feet out to downtown Vancouver, across Georgia Strait to the Gulf Island and Vancouver Island, and south to the Olympic Peninsula. Neighbouring Cypress Bowl, with 14 downhill runs, and Mount Seymour, with 15 runs, have good cross-country trails as well. Cypress and Grouse are lit for night skiing until 22.00 hrs. All three mountains have equipment rentals and restaurants. Spring skiing is usually the best. Hemlock Valley, east in the Fraser Valley, and Whistler/Blackcomb, farther north, are also popular ski areas (see **Excursions from Vancouver**, page 39).

Tennis Vancouver has more than 200 outdoor public tennis courts. All are free and operate on a first come, first serve basis, except for Stanley Park where there is a court fee in summer. The Stanley Park Open tennis tournament takes place mid-July. For locations of public courts, call the Parks Board (tel: 681-1141).

Water Sports

Canoeing and Kayaking Deep Cove Canoe Rentals (tel: 929-2268; open summer only) rent canoes for paddling around Indian Arm, a half-hour drive from downtown. Ecomarine (tel: 689-7575), on Granville Island, rents kayaks all year round. An hour's rental at a reasonable price provides a great seal's eye view of False Creek.

Fishing You must first obtain a fishing licence (either saltwater or freshwater or both), available from major downtown department stores and sporting goods shops. Local sea waters harbour salmon (chinook, coho, chum, pink and sockeye), cod, flounder, snapper and sole, while fresh water offers trout along with the land-locked kokanee salmon. On chartered fishing trips everything is looked after; or you can rent a motorboat (rental fee is by the hour, including insurance). The Barbary Coast Yacht Basin, in Coal Harbour (tel: 669-0088), and Sewell's Landing, in Horseshoe Bay (tel: 921-7461), offer chartered trips and bareboat rentals. For more information, call the Department of Fisheries (tel: 666-2268).

Sailing and Windsurfing The Cooper Blue Orca Boating Centre (tel: 683-6300), on Granville Island, maintains a fleet of 45 sailboats, varying from a 20-foot (7m) sloop to a 48-foot (16m) ketch. Skippered and bareboat rentals are available all year. Windsure Windsurfing, at 1300 Discovery Street (tel: 224-0615), rents boards and wet suits; open 1 April to 30 September.

Scuba Diving The underwater world around Vancouver harbours a great diversity of life: wolf eels and sharks around the Gulf Islands; sea anemones, seals and octopuses in the

Sport in Vancouver gains as much from the spectacular views as from the activity itself

SPORT

underwater reserve at Whytecliff Park; and shipwrecks offshore from Lund. When the plankton dies off in autumn, visibility runs up to 100 feet (30m). Enquire about charter dives at The Diving Locker (tel: 736-2681), Diver's World (tel: 732-1344) and Adrenalin Sports (tel: 682-2881).

Swimming The beaches ringing English Bay offer good swimming in summer. Saltwater pools at Second Beach in Stanley Park and Kitsilano beach are open in June, July and August. Indoor pools at the UBC Aquatic Centre (tel: 228-4521), the Vancouver Aquatic Centre (tel: 665-3424), and the YMCA, at 955 Burrard Street (tel: 681-0221), are open day and evening all through the year.

Spectator Sports

For spectator sports, there are the Vancouver Canucks ice hockey team, the BC Lions football team, the Vancouver 86ers soccer team and the Vancouver Canadians AAA baseball team (one step below Major League standard). Contact the Travel InfoCentre (tel: 683-2000) for details on seasons, game times and locales. The horse racing season at Exhibition Park, at Hastings and Renfrew Streets in east Vancouver (tel: 254-1631), runs mid-April to mid-October; betting diners can watch the races on closed-circuit television.

A moment of high tension in a football game – a very popular sport

DIRECTORY

Arriving

A dozen international airlines serve Vancouver, with regularly scheduled flights from Europe, Asia, the South Pacific, the US, Mexico and South America. Vancouver International Airport and Canada Customs and Immigration can be overloaded in summer and at Christmas and Easter, particularly when a jumbo jet arrives, so relax and enjoy a leisurely arrival. Visitors first go through immigration formalities and then collect checked baggage. Although there are no porters, there are complimentary baggage carts. Customs and immigration regulations are strict and baggage may be searched. Canada does not permit importation of fruit and animal products. There is no inbound duty-free shop. Up one level from the international arrivals area are several car rental offices, a currency exchange counter and a Travel InfoCentre, with a selection of brochures on Vancouver, Victoria and the rest of British Columbia.

Transport to the City Centre

Vancouver Airport is a 30-minute drive from downtown. Taxis cost about C$20 for the trip downtown. Airport Express buses (tel: 261-2299) leave from Level II (Domestic Arrivals), every 15 minutes most of the year, and stop at major downtown hotels and the Greyhound Bus Depot; cost is about C$8 per person.

Camping

Camping is a great way to enjoy the fresh air and natural beauty of British Columbia, especially in summer. The **Capilano Campground** (tel: 987-4722), a 10-minute drive across the Lion's Gate Bridge from the city centre, must be one of the best urban camping areas in the world (see **Accommodation**, page 83). Scattered throughout suburban Vancouver are dozens of other campgrounds, including **Burnaby Cariboo RV Park** (tel: 420-1722), **Park Canada RV Inn** (tel: 943-5811) in Tsawwassen, **Richmond RV Park** (tel: 270-7878) and **KOA Vancouver** (tel: 594-6156) in Surrey. **Porteau Cove Provincial Park** (tel: 898-3678) overlooks Howe Sound, the most southerly fiord in North America. For further information on camping, request the Super Camping booklet from Tourism BC, which lists private campgrounds, BC Parks and motorhome dealers.

Car Breakdown see Driving

Chemist see Pharmacist

Consulates

Embassies are located in Ottawa, Canada's capital, but the following countries (among others) have consulates in Vancouver:

Australia: 602-999 Canada Place (tel: 684-2191)
Britain: 800, 1111 Melville Street (tel: 683-4421)
New Zealand: 1260, 701 West Georgia Street (tel: 684-7388)
United States: 1075 West Georgia Street (tel: 685-4311)

Crime

Vancouver is still relatively safe, compared with such big cities as London and New York. While there appears to be more crime in downtown eastside, caution and common sense are good watchwords everywhere. Stay in well-lit areas and where there are lots of people, and keep a watchful eye on purses, wallets, jewellery and camera equipment. Report any theft immediately to hotel and police.

Customs Regulations

Duty-free allowances for visitors 19 and older (16 and older for tobacco products) are: 200 cigarettes or 50 cigars or 2.2 pounds (1kg) of tobacco; 40 fluid ounces (1.14 litres) of liquor or wine or 24 × 12 fluid ounces (336 mls) cans or bottles of beer or ale, or its equivalent of 288 fluid ounces (8.2 litres); and other dutiable goods to a limit of C$200.
There is no duty on personal belongings for use during your stay.
Gifts valued at more than C$40 are subject to duty and tax on the excess amount; they must not include alcohol, tobacco products or advertising material. Personal funds of C$5,000 or more must be declared.
Revolvers, pistols and fully automatic firearms are prohibited entry into Canada. Quarantine regulations are strict. Plants, bulbs, seeds, fruits and vegetables must be declared and inspected by Agriculture Canada; domestic dogs and cats may be imported without quarantine from rabies-free countries.
Visitors are not allowed to work or study in Canada unless authorization was obtained before entry into the country.

Disabled

Many major hotels and attractions in Vancouver are wheelchair accessible. For information on facilities for physically handicapped travellers, contact any Travel InfoCentre, or request the *Easy Going* booklet from the **Canadian Paraplegic Association**, at 780 South West Marine Drive, BC V6P 5Y7 (tel: 324-3611).

Driving

Gas Gas or petrol is sold by the litre and comes in three grades

of octane. All gas sold is
unleaded (since December
1990).

Regulations Driving is always to
the right, with passing on the left.
The use of seat belts is
mandatory. Right turns are
permitted at red lights, after your
vehicle has come to a full stop.
Road speed limits are 31 mph
(50 kmh) on city roads; 49 mph
(80 kmh) on rural highways; and
62 mph (100 kmh) on major
highways.

More than 80 per cent of the
people who travel in British
Columbia are motorists.
Although Vancouver has more
than its share of traffic accidents,
serious traffic jams are,
fortunately, rare.

Car Breakdown The British
Columbia Automobile
Association honours
memberships from other
automobile associations around
the world. For emergency road
service in the Vancouver area,
call 293-2222.

Your motoring club card is also
good for discounts at numerous
hotels and attractions throughout
the province; request the CAA
discount when making
reservations. For recorded
information on various highway
conditions, call 660-9775.

Car Rental Renting a car is
relatively inexpensive. Major car
rental companies in the
Vancouver area include:
Avis (tel: 682-1621)
Budget (tel: 685-0536)
Hertz (tel: 688-2411)
Tilden (tel: 685-611)
A major credit card is required
to rent a car (otherwise a
passport), even if you plan to pay
in cash. Insurance is usually

*One of the more unusual traffic
hazards to watch out for on the roads:
a wild sheep*

extra, but the Visa Gold Card,
among others, provides free car
insurance; if you are planning to
rent a car for a few weeks, it's
worth investing in a gold credit
card if you qualify. The minimum
age to rent a car can be 25, but
is usually 21 with a major credit
card. Most of the companies
listed, along with several others,
also rent campervans,
motorhomes and four-wheel
drive vehicles. Chauffeured
limousines and other vehicles
are also available. **Exotic Car
Rentals** (tel: 644-9128) have

DIRECTORY

Cyclists come in all shapes and sizes in Vanier Park

available such luxurious vehicles as Porsches, Ferraris and Jaguars. For the other end of the scale, try **Cheapo** (tel: 521-3862) and **Rent-A-Wreck** (tel: 688-0001). Rental companies charge almost double to fill up the tank, so it is best to fill it up before returning the car. Most rented cars use lead-free fuel.

Electricity
Canada's electricity supply is an alternating current of 110 volts at a frequency of 60 cycles. An adaptor is required for most overseas appliances. Adaptors are sold in some hotel shops and at Gulliver's Travel Accessory Stores in Park Royal and Sinclair Centre shopping centres.

Emergency Telephone Numbers
Ambulance: 911 or 0 for operator
Coast Guard Marine: 666-7888
Dental service: contact your hotel concierge, or the
Brentwood Dental Group (tel: 299-7505)
Fire and rescue: 911 or 0
Police: 911 or 0
Prescription Service: contact your hotel concierge, or St Paul's Hospital (tel: 682-2344).
RCMP Freeway Patrol: 666-5343

Entry Formalities
A valid passport (but not a British Visitor's Passport) is required, except for citizens of the US. You must also have a return or onward ticket and evidence of adequate funds for the duration of your visit. Visas are not required for citizens of Britain, Eire, Australia, New Zealand and the US. Persons under 18 years who are not accompanied by an adult must bring a letter from a parent or guardian with permission for them to travel to Canada.

Health Regulations
No vaccinations are required for entry into Canada. Tap water is safe to drink anywhere in the

country; however, if you are camping, it is wise to boil water from lakes and rivers. Canadian health care standards are high. If you become ill, ask your hotel to recommend a nearby physician. Medical insurance to cover the duration of your stay in Canada is recommended, as medical services are expensive.

Hire Facilities

Bicycles Cycling around Stanley Park and other areas of Vancouver is a wonderful way to see the city and savour the sights. Contact Stanley Park Rentals (tel: 681-5581), at the Georgia Street entrance to the park, or check the yellow pages of the Vancouver telephone directory.

Boats Sailing boats, motorboats and houseboats are available for rent from dozens of companies both in and outside Vancouver. Call the nearest Travel InfoCentre for details.

Camping Equipment Rudy's Sporting Goods, at 3279 West Broadway (tel: 731-5122), rents tents, sleeping bags, air mattresses, backpacks, stoves, boots, crampons and other sporting goods.

Cars see **Car Rentals**, page 111.

Holidays

There are 10 statutory holidays in British Columbia. Banks, post offices, liquor stores, government and most offices and many stores are closed on these holidays. City buses operate on a reduced schedule.

New Year's Day: 1 January
Good Friday: late March/April
Easter Monday: late March/April
Victoria Day: 24 May or the preceding Monday

Canada Day: 1 July
British Columbia Day: first Monday in August
Labour Day: first Monday in September
Thanksgiving Day: second Monday in October
Remembrance Day: 11 November
Christmas Day: 25 December
Boxing Day: 26 December

Schools are closed during July and August, for 10 days in March or April for Easter or spring break, and for two weeks in late December and early January.

Lost Property

Vancouver does not have a central Lost Property office. It is best to check with the nearest police station. For property left on trains, ferries, buses or taxis, call the company's head office.

Media

Print Although the best daily in the country, the morning *Globe & Mail*, has limited local news, *The Province*, a morning tabloid, and *The Vancouver Sun*, a mid-day broadsheet, both cover the city scene thoroughly. All three are available at news stands and in street coin boxes. The weekly *Westender* (published Thursdays) and the *Georgia Straight* provide compact coverage of entertainment and are available at no charge at newsstands or hotels. The monthly *Key to Vancouver*, also available free in hotels and for a dollar in street coin boxes, is especially for visitors and includes information on shopping, dining, attractions, entertainment, special events, maps and evening television programming. Such local glossy monthly magazines as *Vancouver*, *Western Living* and *West* include articles of local interest.

Electronic Favourite local radio stations include CBC at 690 AM and 105.7 FM (talk and classical music with no commercials); CKNW at 980; (talk, middle-of-the-road music and sports); and CHQM at 1320 AM and LITE 1320 (easy listening).

Local television stations include CBC-TV (Canadian Broadcasting Corporation) on Cable 3, BCTV (the CTV network) on Cable 11 and the Knowledge Network (the British Columbia educational channel) on Cable 5. Dozens of other channels, including PBS, ABC, CBS and NBC from the US, are also available in Vancouver. Check the listings which are given at the back of *Key to Vancouver* magazine.

Money Matters

Currency Canada has a decimal currency system with 100 cents to the dollar. Coins are one cent, five cents (a nickel), 10 cents (a dime), 25 cents (a quarter), 50 cents (half-dollar) and the one-dollar coin commonly known as a Loonie. The bills are colour-coded: $1 is green, $2 is brown, $5 is blue, $10 is purple, $20 is green, $50 is red and $100 is beige. Merchants don't like to give up a lot of change, so $100 notes are not popular; $20 notes always seem to be acceptable.

Money Exchange Most foreign currencies and travellers' cheques can be exchanged at the foreign exchange counters at the airport, at major city banks and at hotels. Other money changers such as Deaks, Money

Canada has a rich heritage of colourful Indian crafts

Express and Money Mart may charge higher commissions and offer less favourable exchange rates. Since exchange rates are subject to fluctuation at the best of times, check the Canadian dollar rates when you arrive in Canada.

Credit Cards such as American Express, Carte Blanche, Diners Club, Mastercard and Visa are accepted in most hotels, restaurants and shops and in some parking lots. Provincial sales tax is six per cent on most merchandise; hotel tax is 10 per cent, and there is a 10 per cent sales tax on all liquor consumed in bars and restaurants.

Opening Times

Banks Regular banking hours are 10.00–16.00 hrs Monday to Friday, often extended to 17.00 hrs on Fridays. A few downtown banks open at 08.00 hrs. Some banks are open on Saturday mornings, but all banks are closed on Sundays and holidays.

Museums, Galleries and Attractions Most are open 10.00–17.00 hrs daily, but some are closed one day a week, and some have extended or shortened hours on certain days.

Post Offices 08.00–17.30 hrs Monday to Friday. Some sub-stations are open Saturday mornings.

Shops Most shops and stores are open 09.30–18.00 hrs Monday to Friday, with extended hours to 21.00 on Thursdays and Fridays. Most are open 09.30–17.30 Saturday and many are open 12.00–17.00 on Sundays. Such corner stores as 7-Eleven are often open 06.00–24.00 hrs and

some are open all night.

Personal Safety

Although Canada's wildlife varies from polar bears to mammoth mosquitoes, Vancouver wildlife is limited to squirrels, raccoons and an occasional mosquito. The North Shore mountains are home to deer, coyotes and black bears. If you see a bear, sing, shout or yodel and if necessary toss a few pebbles towards it. The bear will probably amble off in seach of more berries in a more serene setting. The only real hazard in Vancouver is rain, which tends to dampen spirits and make sightseeing a little soggy.

Pharmacist

Medical prescriptions in British Columbia are available only through a local doctor. Many pharmacies are hidden at the back of big drugstores. Drugstores sell non-prescription medication in great abundance. **Shoppers Drug Mart**, at 1160 Robson Street (tel: 681-8177), and **London Drugs**, at 1187 Robson Street (tel: 669-7374), are open Monday to Saturday 09.00–22.00 hrs and 10.00–20.00 hrs on Sundays.

Photography

Print film, which is inexpensive and sold almost everywhere, from variety shops to grocery stores, can be developed within an hour or two at numerous photo shops. Slide film, sold primarily in photo shops, takes 24 hours to develop, except for Kodachrome, which takes a week. **CustomColor**, at 1110 Robson Street (tel: 681-2524), provides reliable service for

DIRECTORY

both prints and slides. Many shops in Vancouver sell disposable cameras.

Places of Worship
Here are a few of the hundreds of places, of many denominations, to worship in and around Vancouver:
Akali Singh Sikh Temple, 1890 Skeena Street (tel: 254-2117)
Beth Israel Synagogue, 4350 Oak Street (tel: 731-4161)
Canadian Memorial United Church, 1811 West Sixteenth Avenue (tel: 731-3101)
Central Presbyterian Church, 1155 Thurlow Street (tel: 683-1913)
Christ Church Anglican Cathedral, 690 Burrard Street (tel: 682-3848)
Christian Science Church, 1160 West Georgia Street (tel: 685-7544)
First Baptist Church, 969 Burrard Street (tel: 683-8441)
Holy Rosary Catholic Cathedral, at Dunsmuir and Richards Streets (tel: 682-6774)
Ismaili Mosque, 4010 Canada Way, Burnaby (tel: 438-4010)
Shia Mosque 3360 Sexsmith, Richmond (tel: 270-3923)

Post Office
The main post office at 349 West Georgia Street is open Monday to Friday 08.00–17.30 hrs. Numerous sub-stations in malls, drugstores and even dry cleaning shops are open on Saturdays as well. Some have stamp, courier and facsimile services.
Postage stamps are also sold in some hotels and tourist shops which sell postcards. Canada post boxes are red. Mail can be sent to you c/o General Delivery

at any post office in Canada. To send a telegram or telepost, call CNCP Telecommunications on 681-4231.

Public Transport

Airlines
Air BC (tel: 278-3800)
Air Canada (tel: 688-5515)
Burrard Air (tel: 662-3479)
Canadian Airlines (tel: 682-1411)
Harbour Air (tel: 688-1277)

Getting around is easy and scenic, whether you go by bus...

Helijet Airways (tel: 273-1414)
Tyee Airways (tel: 689-8651)
Vancouver Helicopters (tel: 525-1484)

Buses
Cascade Coach Lines (tel: 662-3222): to the Fraser Valley
Gray Line (tel: 681-8687): sightseeing tours
Greyhound (tel: 662-3222): throughout Canada
Maverick Coach Lines (tel: 255-1171): to Nanaimo, Sunshine Coast, Squamish, Whistler and Pemberton
Perimeter Transportation (tel: 273-9023): between downtown

and the airport

BC Transit (tel: 261-5100):
Vancouver's regional transit
system, which includes buses,
the SeaBus and the SkyTrain,
runs along major arteries
throughout city centre and
suburbs. There are three peak
time fare zones in Greater
Vancouver. Day passes are
available for children, adults and
seniors. Exact change is
required, but tickets and passes
are sold at 7-Eleven and at other
convenience stores and
drugstores. Transit timetables
are available from public
libraries, city and municipal
halls, Travel InfoCentres and BC
Transit offices and terminals.
The SeaBuses, which are
actually 400-passenger
catamaran ferries, make the 15-
minute trip across Burrard Inlet
to North Vancouver every 15
minutes (fewer sailings in the
evenings and on Sundays).
Unfortunately, they have no
outside decks, but the views are
still spectacular. The SkyTrain
runs 14 miles (22km) from
Canada Place downtown to New
Westminster, with 17 stops *en
route*. Most of the line is
elevated, so the trip is scenic
when the sun is shining. Trains
run every five minutes.

Ferries

The little Aquabus Ferries from
the foot of Hornby Street and the
False Creek ferries from the
Aquatic Centre run to and from
Granville Island seven days a
week, all year round. **BC Ferries**
(tel: 685-1021), which carry
vehicles and foot passengers,
run from Tsawwassen (an hour's
drive south from city centre) to

*… or by train, taking advantage of a
BC Rail day round-trip*

Swartz Bay (a half-hour from
Victoria) on Vancouver Island
and to the Gulf Islands. From the
other ferry terminal at
Horseshoe Bay (a half-hour drive
northwest from downtown),
ferries sail to Nanaimo, Bowen
Island and the Sunshine Coast.

Trains

BC Rail (tel: 984-5264) operates
daily round-trip rail service from
North Vancouver via Squamish,
Whistler and Pemberton to
Lillooet. BC Rail also runs trains
thrice-weekly (summer only) to
Prince George via Clinton, 100-
Mile House, Quesnel and

Williams Lake. **Via Rail** (tel: 800-561-8630) operates some passenger services across Canada, departing from the station on Main Street.

Taxis
It's hard to hail a cab in downtown Vancouver, especially in the pouring rain when you need one most. Best to head to the nearest big hotel, where taxis usually wait in line, or phone any of the following:
Black Top (tel: 681-2181)
MacLures (tel: 683-6666)
Yellow Cab (tel: 681-1111)

Senior Citizens
Those over 65 years of age are eligible to reductions on air, rail and bus fares. Numerous hotels, stores, attractions and events offer reduced rates for seniors 50 or older, although 'Seniors' generally means at least 65. Bring an ID card which indicates your birth date. Among Vancouver hotels that

offer discounts to seniors are the **Hyatt Regency** (50 per cent off all year round, space available); the **Park Royal** (20 per cent off, May to September) and the **Westin Bayshore** (50 per cent off mid-October to mid-April, 20–25 per cent the rest of the year). Many restaurants in Vancouver and throughout the province offer 10–20 per cent discounts for seniors. Such restaurant chains as **Bino's**, **Denny's** and **White Spot** list small-portion dishes for seniors. Others advertise discounts on early evening dining. Such restaurants as the elegant **Forster's**, in Emerald Park, North Vancouver (tel: 988-8353), knock as much as 20 per cent off regular menu prices. **Troll's** restaurants, renowned for fantastic fish and chips, offer a 10 per cent

If travelling at ground-level bores you, try flying along in the Grouse Mountain cable car

discount off full meals and also list half-order lunch and dinner specials. Senior citizens who like their fish really fresh can buy fishing licences at reduced prices. **Como Lake**, in suburban Coquitlam, has been set aside for anglers aged 65 and older (and youngsters under 16). Harbour Ferries, Granville Island Ferries, city buses, the SeaBus, the SkyTrain and BC Rail all offer reduced fares for seniors. And domestic airlines frequently feature special promotions for seniors on flights throughout the province and across Canada; call the companies directly for details. Such attractions as the **Dr Sun Yat Sen Chinese Garden**, the **Vancouver Art Gallery**, the **Museum of Anthropology**, the **Maritime Museum**, **Science World**, the **Imax** show, the **Bloedel Conservatory** and **Grouse Mountain** all advertise reduced admission for seniors. Seniors also get a break at the **Vancouver Aquarium**. It is best to go in the afternoon, though, for mornings are often crowded with school children. The **Vancouver Aquatic Centre**, on Tuesday and Thursday mornings, offers a seniors' programme which includes exercises on the deck and in the pool. The Centre also organizes daytrips to such places as Horseshoe Bay and Victoria and such special events as Valentine Tea.

The Vancouver Symphony, city cinemas and theatres offer reduced rates to seniors, occasionally by as much as 80 per cent.

There's no harm in asking about a seniors' discount while shopping. Some groceries, drugstores and department stores reduce prices by 10–15 per cent one day a month for seniors.

Travel-wise seniors get a great break on BC vacations through **Elderhostel**, 300, 33 Prince Arthur Avenue, Toronto, Ontario M5R 1B2, which offers 70 different study options in 11 centres throughout the province, including Harbour House on Saltspring Island, Strathcona Park Lodge, and Twin Island Resort near Salmon Arm. A monthly publication, *The Elder Statesman* (tel: 683-1344), provides more information especially for seniors.

Student and Youth Travel

Many attractions and events in the Vancouver area offer reduced rates for students. Bring your student card. People between 13 and 21 can get reduced rates by air and rail if they provide proof of age.

Telephones

Public telephones are located in post offices, hotel lobbies, public buildings and in phone booths throughout the city. Some public phones are specifically for long-distance calls, and some are designated for credit card use only.

Both local and international calls are usually more expensive on hotel phones. The area code for British Columbia is 604. International calls from Canada can be dialled direct using the codes: Britain 01 44; Eire 01 353; Australia 01/61; New Zealand 01 64, follwed by the area code (dropping the initial 0) and the

DIRECTORY

number. For the US dial the area code and number.

Ticket Agencies

The **Vancouver Travel InfoCentre**, at 1055 Dunsmuir Street (tel: 683-2000), makes hotel reservations and sells theatre, sports, sightseeing and BC Transit tickets. It also has a currency exchange and sells stamps, film, souvenirs, guide books and posters.

For such major events as opera, symphony, ballet, theatre, sports and rock concerts and some attractions, call **Ticketmaster** on 280-4444. By telephone you can pay with American Express, Mastercard or Visa; at counters scattered throughout city shopping malls, you can pay wih credit cards or cash. Cinema tickets are sold only at individual theatres; for show times at **Cineplex Odeon**, call 687-1515.

Time

Most of British Columbia is on Pacific Standard Time, which in summer is nine hours behind GMT. Clocks fall back an hour on the last Sunday in October and spring forward on the first Sunday in April. Vancouver time is three hours behind Toronto time and four hours behind New York. For most of the year, Vancouver is 18 hours behind Sydney and 20 hours behind New Zealand.

Tipping

Canadians usually tip 10 to 20 per cent in restaurants and bars and for taxis. Sometimes a higher tip reflects better service, but Canadians unfortunately are reluctant to reduce tips for bad service. Service might improve if customers consistently tipped more for superior service. Tipping is optional for porters, doormen, chambermaids and other service personnel.

Toilets

Public toilets are located in railway, bus, SeaBus and SkyTrain terminals, and in shopping centres and department stores. If you're desperate and there are no public toilets around, politely ask a nearby hotel, bar or restaurant if you may use theirs.

Tourist Information

For advance information on Vancouver and most parts of British Columbia, contact the following information centres:

Canada: Vancouver Travel InfoCentre, 1055 Dunsmuir Street, Vancouver, BC V7X 1L3, Canada (tel: 604/683-2000)

UK: Tourism BC, 1 Regent Street, London SW1Y 4NS (tel: 930-6857)

US: Tourism BC, Suite 1050, 2600 Michelson Drive, Irvine, California 90010 (tel: (714) 852-1054)

Australia: Tourism Canada, AMP Centre, 50 Bridge Street, Sydney NSW, Australia 2000 (tel: 231-6522)

New Zealand: Canadian High Commission, ICI House, 67 Molesworth Street, Wellington, New Zealand (tel: 739-577)

Tours

Visitors can see Vancouver and environs by foot, by bicycle, by boat (canoe, kayak, motorboat or yatcht), by bus or limousine or Model A Ford, and by plane, helicopter or hot air balloon. While North American travellers tend to be do-it-yourself sightseers or rely on VFR (visiting friends and relatives) tours, many commercial tours are available, although some operate only in summer.

Air Tours
Harbour Air (tel: 688-1277) packages seven seaplane tours, varying from a half-hour flight over city centre to the Princess Louisa Inlet Tour, which includes a stopover for lunch beside a wilderness waterfall.
West Wind Balloon Tours (tel: 530-1633) offers the ultimate romantic adventure in a drift along with the breeze over the verdant Fraser Valley; a traditional champagne celebration tops the flight, after landing.
Vancouver Helicopter Tours (tel: 683-HELI) provides scenic city and wilderness sightseeing;

options vary from a 20-minute flight over English Bay, Stanley Park and the Lion's Gate Bridge to the 90-minute Coastal Mountain Odyssey, which includes a short stopover on a glacier.

Bicycle Tours
The **Bicycling Association of British Columbia** (tel: 731-7433) welcomes non-members to join their city cycling and farther afield trips, for both leisurely touring and technical training camps.

Bus and Car Tours
Gray Line (tel: 681-8687) and **Pacific Coach Lines** (tel: 662-7575) offer several sightseeing tours. Itineraries range from a simple downtown circuit and a

Seaplane tours provide a different view of the city sights

four-hour evening tour, including a sampling of Cantonese cuisine, to a seven-day return ride through the Canadian Rockies to Calgary. The Gray Line city morning tour sometimes includes the bonus of veteran broadcaster Bill Hughes, who has talked to more than 300,000 city visitors for CKNW Radio's *Roving Mike*, listed as the world's longest running radio broadcast in the *Guinness Book of Records*. **Early Motion Tours** (tel: 687-5088) proffer the luxury of a finely tuned original 1928 or 1930 Model A Ford Phaeton touring car. Tours can be tailored to your tastes and include a framed Polaroid photo of you and the Phaeton.
Classic Limousine Service (tel: 669-5466) offers custom-designed tours in the luxury of a limousine, day or night, all year round.

Historical Walking Tours
Vancouver historian **Chuck Davis** (tel: 583-2920), who probably knows Vancouver past and present better than anyone, tailors walking tours of city centre to your interests.

Train Tours
Harbour Tours (tel: 688-7246) provides a ride back to the past aboard the historic *Royal Hudson* steam train to Squamish, with an optional return aboard the MV Britannia; operates summer only.

Water Tours
Gray Line (tel: 681-8687) and the **SS *Beaver*** (tel: 682-7284) offer harbour sightseeing tours. The SS *Beaver* Indian Arm excursion includes a mesquite grilled

salmon lunch. Both Gray Line and the SS *Beaver*, along with **Bayshore Yacht Charters** (tel: 691-6016), offer three-hour dinner cruises; salmon and a spectacular sunset are likely to be part of the evening menu.
Bayshore Yacht Charters, along with **Sewell's Marina** (tel: 921-7461), in Horseshoe Bay, offer skippered fishing tours.
For whitewater adventure, May to September, call **Hyak** (tel: 734-8622), who guided National Geographic down the Chilko-Chilcotin Rivers. Their Rapids Transist System runs from downtown to the Chilliwack, Thomson and Chilko Rivers, where they lead you through rushing whitewater in inflatable rafts or kayaks.

For a close look at some elegant boats, take a harbour tour

LANGUAGE

While Canada is a bilingual country, with English and French as official languages, English is the usual language of business in provinces outside Quebec. In Vancouver, Cantonese is more common than French, but you are apt to hear many languages, varying from Chinook to Vietnamese. The English language in Canada is a product of social, ethnic and historical factors. British settlers in the 19th century naturally brought their language with them and some older English words remain. Early American prospectors and pioneers, along with the modern influences of American media and advertising, have also played a role in the development of Canadian English. Fur traders, homesteaders and the continuing influx of immigrants from around the world have all contributed to the variations in the English vocabulary that occur in this country.

The following glossary lists common Canadian words and expressions; some are most familiar to British Columbians and Vancouverites.

Anglophone English-speaking person

apartment flat

awesome as in 'totally awesome'; favoured by the younger set

baby carriage pram

back of, in back of behind (a remnant of 18th-century British English)

back forty the far end of a lot (from 19th-century prairie homesteaders)

bannock Indian bread

bar a drinking place, and also a ridge of sand or gravel in a stream or river where gold may be found by panning, as in Boston Bar

blueberry tea a strong alcoholic drink

BC Tel The British Columbia Telephone Company, the major telephone system in the province

bush wilderness

CBC the Canadian Broadcasting System, in Vancouver located at the corner of Hamilton and Georgia Streets, which operates radio stations and television channels in English and French throughout Canada

can tin

LANGUAGE

candy sweets

Canuck slang for Canadian; the local hockey team is called the Vancouver Canucks

chinook mature spring salmon

chum dog salmon, called *qualla* (striped) by the Indians

coho Salish Indian word for silver salmon or fall fish

cookie biscuit

cop policeman

cut-throat a kind of trout

dim sum Chinese breakfast or lunch

Dene Indian people

Dome the BC Place Stadium

Dolly Varden a char with olive skin and red spots, so named by a literary angler who was reminded of Barnaby Rudge's flowery dress, created by Charles Dickens

elevator lift

fender wing

fish ladder a series of upward levels built in a river or stream to help salmon return to spawning grounds

forest reserve an area set aside for controlled logging

Francophone French-speaking Canadian

garbage can dust bin

gas petrol

generator dynamo

hockey usually means ice hockey

hurdy gurdy a dance hostess in the Cariboo gold mining era (comes from the British 'barrel organ')

hydro hydro electric

Indian summer a pleasant, warm period, usually following the first cold days of autumn

Inuit Eskimo

inukshuk man-shaped cairn believed to have spiritual powers; there's one in Vancouver's West End, overlooking English Bay

Inuktitut language of the Inuit

kayak a low, light canoe, closed to keep the water out; now made from fibreglass, originally made from animal skins

Kits short for Kitsilano, a yuppie residential area close to downtown with many shops and restaurants

kokanee land-locked salmon, and a local beer

Labrador tea infusion from leaves of the Labrador plant

log boom an assembly of logs in water ready to be tugged to another area

logging lumbering

lumber timber

mile houses hotels whose locations were measured in miles from Yale, head of navigation of the Fraser River during the 1858 gold rush.

Mountie RCMP officer

mukluks Inuit boots, originally made from sealskin

Ogopogo mythical monster in Okanagan Lake

oolichan Indian name for candle fish; some say the little fish is so oily that it can be lit on one end and used as a candle

parka a warm jacket, usually hooded

panning separating gold from gravel by washing in a pan

pan out turn out well

portage carry canoes and cargo around such obstructions as rapids

potlatch originally an Indian festival where gifts were distributed, but now merely a festival

province a political division of Canada

RCMP Royal Canadian Mounted Police

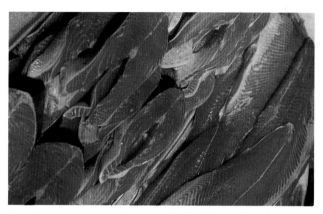

If you have a particular taste for salmon, Vancouver's menus should fit the bill

Rocky Mountain oysters fried calf testicles

saltchucker anyone who fishes in the sea for sport

saltchuck ocean

sashimi Japanese appetiser of thin slices of raw fish

sasquatch legendary big wild hairy man of the mountains, similar to the Yeti (abominable snowman) of the Himalayas and the American Bigfoot

shivaree a noisy celebration, originally taking place after a wedding

skookum strong or great (from the Chinook language), as in 'That's skookum, man!' (That's great!)

snuck up sneaked up

slough a swamp or bog; rhymes with 'you'

slug in city bars slang for a single drink; in the rainforest, a gigantic snail without a shell

sockeye a kind of West Coast salmon (from the Salish *suk-kegh*, meaning red fish)

Stanley Cup a national hockey trophy for the best team of the season

Socred Social Credit political party, popular in British Columbia

tillicum Indian word for person or friend

totem a carved cedar pole of symbolic figures, sometimes painted

tuque a French Canadian knitted winter cap, tapered at one end

tyee chinook salmon weighing more than 28 pounds (13kg); means 'chief' or 'big' in the Indian Language

undershirt vest

vest waistcoat

wants in/wants out wants to come in and go out

whiskey jack Canada jay (comes from the Cree *wisketjan*)

West End cluster of high-rise apartments situated between downtown, Stanley Park and English Bay

West Van West Vancouver, located across the Lion's Gate Bridge, northwest of Vancouver and west of North Vancouver.

INDEX

INDEX/ACKNOWLEDGEMENTS

The Automobile Association would like to thank the following photographers and libraries for their assistance in the preparation of this book:

MICHAEL DENT took all the photographs in this book (© AA Photo Library) except:

J ALLAN CASH PHOTO LIBRARY 12/13 Lion's Gate Bridge, 16 Totem in Museum of Anthropology, 103 Fireworks.

BRITISH COLUMBIA HOUSE Cover Canada Place, 117 Rail Dayliner.

NATURE PHOTOGRAPHERS LTD 65 Bunchberry (A J Cleave), 66 Harlequin (P R Sterry), 67 Wapati (D A Smith).

SPECTRUM COLOUR LIBRARY 49 Kootenay National Park.

ZEFA PICTURE LIBRARY UK LTD 4 Vancouver skyline, 41 Rockies, 54 Okanagen Lake, 58 Black bear, 61 Beaver, 62 Salmon, 68 Humpback whale, 84/5 At night, 87 Science World at night, 107 Katamaran.